LIVING GOD BLUES

BY THE SAME AUTHOR

Spiritual Slavery

Beyond Release

In The Fire

Laughter of the Stones

Zen Gamesmanship: The Art of Bridge

The Cheating Buddha

The Yoga of Enlightenment/
The Book of Unenlightenment

Acting God...

The Only Grace is Loving God

LIVING GOD BLUES

by Lee Lozowick

HOHM PRESS
Prescott Valley, Arizona
1 9 8 4

Manufactured in the United States of America.
International Standard Book Number: 0-934252-09-2
Published by Hohm Press, P.O. Box 26403,
Prescott Valley, Arizona 86312

PREFACE

This book might reveal to you the unexpected. Beware of what the "words" do to you—they are only vehicles. Do not look just at the container; look at what it contains.

There is a tendency today to mistake the message for the messenger, the play for the player, the dance for the dancer, the Teaching for the Teacher. But at this time in our human evolution, it has become essential to shift the focus toward the invisible messages which are being embodied in, or manifested by, the visible beings we call "Teachers." By transfering our attention from appearance to essence, we can open the road and widen the path.

So, read between the lines in this book, and search for the obvious — that which is quite elusive to many. Make use of Lee's language to help you become aware of that devious now so that the future will continue to be present.

Turn the page. Open the window. Live long and prosper.

Samuel Avital, founder and director
Le Centre du Silence Mime School
Boulder, Colorado

FOREWORD

Three weeks ago my girlfriend and I decided to go to Phoenix to visit her mother and get away from the New York spring storms. I didn't tell Saqi I was going to be in his neighborhood because I wanted to surprise him with a phone call from Phoenix, as I had on New Year's day. One of the things I looked forward to was visiting the ashram in Prescott again. But when I called, the surprise was mine, for Saqi told me he was just about to leave for Tucson to work in a street fair. I told him I'd drop by to see him there the next afternoon.

By the way the world measures such things, Saqi is a successful spiritual master. He has some twenty or twenty-five completely committed devotees, scores of disciples and students, and thousands of admirers. His community in Arizona is prospering and he's published half a dozen books or more. He could be much "bigger" if he were willing to compromise his message or at least present it in a slicker package. And even as things are, he could be taking it easy, the way most *arriviste gurus* do, by removing himself from the textures and demands of daily life and only making formal meditative appearances from time to time. Instead, he embodies all the relationships and labors that he requires of others, including — as he was doing in Tucson — spending several days in a tiny wooden booth cooking and selling food at a street fair.

For the seven years I've known Saqi, I've always respected the way he goes about being a spiritual master, but I've never been able to buy into his trip. I've bowed at his feet in darshan and tried to feel what "surrender" to him might be, but there was not the slightest resonance to that process anywhere in my being. Also, I'm at odds with his rhetoric. He teaches "Loving God" and I'm not sure I even like God very much.

However, despite — and perhaps because of — the gap between our stated worldviews, we've developed a friendship.

So, as my girlfriend and I drove south to Tucson the following morning, I wondered at what our meeting would be like this time, curious as to what balance would be struck between the formal relationship of our philosophical personae and our organic old-boy feeling for one another. Magdalena and I found the street fair, and walked around for some time before I finally spotted the Fry Bread booth, almost entirely hidden by another stand at the end of a dead-end street. Inside were Saqi and four of his devotees busy at various tasks — making and kneading dough, tending vats of boiling oil, chopping vegetables, stirring beans, serving customers. They worked with quiet intensity. Saqi exuded an air of timelessness and it was easy to picture him as a tailor in medieval Morocco or a weaver in Persia, appearing in different cultures in different costumes but always with the same role and function — an anonymous man in the marketplace who cannot be distinguished from others by any visible sign but whose presence bespeaks divine absorption. There was something quintessentially Sufic in the moment.

We walked up to the booth and peered through the thick wire mesh that hangs at eye level over the counter, and I shouted a hello. Saqi looked up from what he was doing and said, by way of a greeting. "So. How would you like to write the introduction to another book?" I was taken aback. The offer was totally unexpected, and such is Saqi's manner that I couldn't be sure whether he'd had the idea earlier and was now communicating it, or whether the notion had just sprung full-blown from his lips without any previous thought. I agreed to do it, but not without ambivalence. A few months earlier I'd made a formal break with all traditional spiritual approaches, even contemporary radical models like Saqi's. I'd just had a book published that offered an alternative. And I was afraid that I'd be forced to choose between writing a polite evasion or a principled refutation.

It was only when I returned to Manhattan that the solution to the potential dilemma occurred to me. I decided that I wouldn't read the manuscript of the book! After all, if I don't know what it says, I can't say anything about it. Although, if it's anything like Saqi's previous works, I'm sure I would wind up arguing with his premises, shaking my head at the flashes of spiritual arrogance that show through the text, and wince at his jokes. In so doing, I would be reacting exactly as he intended, for he uses words as goads to piss people off and make them uncomfortable, on the grounds that only such a condition will make them question the nature of their existence and consider the possibility of "real" spiritual life and community.

So I am ignorant of what you'll be reading on the pages that follow. But the two things I do know about the book I can recommend unqualifiedly. One is the author, who plays just about the best game of spiritual hardball anywhere. And the other is the title. In line with populist theocracy these days, it states that God is not Dead, but Living (Hallelujah). But in his inimitable way, Saqi goes on to note that this God has got the Blues, a proposition that makes a great deal of sense to me. Given the abysmal quality of the human condition, God *should* be down.

Perhaps it is only when the divine comes off it, and gets down with us folk, that the existence of the divine has any meaning. They say that's what Jesus was about. I know that that's what Saqi is about.

Marco Vassi
April 1984
New York City

The Editors

The first section of this book was compiled and edited by senior students in the Hohm Community. It is the first in-depth elucidation of the Teaching of our spiritual Master Lee Lozowick and describes the process his students have been involved in with him over the last nine years.

Lee Lozowick awakened to his function as spiritual Master in July of 1975 and the Hohm Community soon formed around him.

It was a wild time, full of the infatuation of the first blush of the truth; an ancient Buddha in the guise of a Jewish meditation teacher, full of decidedly "unBuddha-like" characteristics, a sangha of middle class, immature, yet wildly enthusiastic "kids," and a dharma of apparently irrational, even nasty communications. Hohm was making its impact, full of noise, partying, and celebration. The first written communication of Lee's realization that nothing was separate from God took the form of *Spiritual Slavery* and it was a raw book, full of expletives, outrageous statements, and an impact that brought hundreds of students seeking his company.

Very few found what they were looking for. He was not a New Age teacher who offered easy solutions to psychological quirks, or a yogi who recommended practices as remedies for illusory ills, or someone with a little energy who could make us feel kundalini.[1] He didn't say to look within, or to serve the world outwardly. He was not even an example of how to be a better human being. His message was, "The work I have come here to do is the same work you have come here to

[1]Kundalini is a form of energy said to rest at the base of the spine (the muladhar chakra), in the form of a coiled snake, which, when awakened, rises up the spinal line opening each chakra in turn, culminating with the opening of the seventh chakra (sahasrar). The opening of the seventh chakra is traditionally equated with the attainment of Enlightenment.

do, I have assumed it, you have not." His only focus was the Will of God, all else was considered irrelevant. He was therefore quite irreverant to those who sought his company expecting a social reformer or a man selling wisdom in worldly ways. Seekers found that which is identical to the Great Process of Divine Evolution: the Godman. And he made the absolute and traditional demand of such a one: surrender, obedience, devotion.

In the Western world we have virtually no education about spiritual life. Most of us didn't even know it existed until adulthood, so we have no preparation for making use of or simply honoring such a being. And that explains why creating a spiritual culture and the proper relationship to a *Godman* is so very difficult. Ancient scriptures tell us that the Godman appears when the world forgets God, when only Help of a Divine kind will avail. When mankind no longer remembers what is holy and sacred, God cannot be communicated to man except in human terms. So, in an age where it is very apparent that man needs help, the element of the Godman is provided in the living form of the spiritual Master. He is born, seemingly like every one of us, yet Lee said early in his new "career," "I am the same One Who has always been, the Man of Life, the Light of the Gods, the Freedom of Creation."

Over the years, Lee's students have questioned him about his personal history, wishing to verify that he was always extraordinary. His response was always that he had almost no memory of being young and that his history was so ordinary it was hardly worth investigating. He always ridiculed our interest in his past as nonsense. He said, "Look at who I am, not the illusion of 'history.' " But recently he has begun to give us more information and it does point to a human condition that was not the usual one. The background of our spiritual Master, when viewed with understanding, describes someone to whom the obviousness of "what is" was always present, to whom there was no dilemma, no problem to life at all.

Lee came from an unusual family. His grandfather, a Russian Jew, was a spiritual Teacher in his own tradition and was known as a Tzaddik.

His father, Louis Lozowick, was one of the master lithographers of the twentieth century. He was full of vitality, a passionate man, passionate about his art and passionate about social and political issues. He was completely dedicated to his art and its *essential* impact and would often refuse to sell his works to private collectors, selling them instead to museums for far less because of his wish that his work be communicated to many people. He was full of information, knowledge, and wisdom, and the household was full of lively discussion with friends on every variety of subject, from art and politics to mysticism and astronomy.

Lee's mother brought an innocence and devotion to husband and son that is uncommon. Lee has described his relationship to his father as one of awe, that to his mother as loving conflict. She is a devotee of her son and has always supported and honored him.

But it is the quality of innocence that both parents provided that is of crucial import. This *is* the environment he chose to be born into. The context of existence as described by Lee is Organic Innocence and it would appear that he "selected" his parents for the particular circumstance in which his own particular expression of the Truth could form.

He describes recognizing as far back as memory began that everything was always obvious and ordinary to him. There was no accompanying identification with the usual formation of personality, habits, tendencies, etc. "Conciousness was always obvious and never changed—everything was just what it was." And this expressed itself as an equilibrium that few understood. Relatives, lovingly yet with some perplexity, referred to Lee as cold hearted. This conflicted with the fact that he was the favorite child of the large and warmly close-knit family. They all loved his company, but in calling him cold hearted, they did show a recognition of his being different—in this case, an inability to be taken in by what wasn't real in others. He never played the conventional social game, while still expressing love in an undeniable way. He lacked other qualities too—jealousy, envy, self importance, and proceeded through childhood and adolescence with the usual bumps and grinds, joys and sorrows, yet without the impulse to alter his life. This equilibrium was barely disturbed until it became necessary for Lee to submit himself to his students and take on all their frustration and anger and pain.

Another aspect that stands out about his youth is the simple ease with which Lee moved through life and interests. His approach was to investigate something until it became obvious, become expert in it to the point of Real Understanding, if not mastery of form, and then move on. As a child, he was absorbed in natural things and collected snakes, bugs, fish, frogs, anything alive. He was *completely* ordinary. Passions did consume him but he didn't form the usual kinds of attachments to things. His idiosyncrasies moved and changed as fluently as the eddies in a stream. When this period of interest in "nature" exhausted itself, he was completely finished with it.

On the surface, such a description of someone would not be significant, but what we're unaware of in most people is the undercurrent of desperation and various neuroses that feed interests or block a natural, easeful passage through them. When Lee describes himself at a young age, you know that he is describing *exactly* what was going on. There were no undercurrents that captured him, but at the same time this doesn't imply a dullness. He had read many of the classics of traditional literature by thirteen and so was very familiar with the human dilemma. He also observed those around him and knew himself to be different. Many of us can remember a certain point in early childhood when we felt we were different from other people, but that implied a very big dilemma and cut us off from others. This recognition was not a problem for Lee. His condition remained that of simply, tacitly recognizing and moving through all that arose. And it remained so until his late twenties when the environment began to describe his state to him.

Lee tells a delightful story of how his best friend in eighth grade wrote an essay using Lee as his subject. The boy spoke of his friend's nose as being a classic type, "the perfect Roman nose," and in that moment Lee was struck by the simple truth that *everything* was perfect. This story is not as simple as it appears. Lee was not in any conventional position to recognize that "everything was perfect." He was immature physically, was laughed at for being different, was not a brilliant student anymore, (he had been prior to thirteen) and didn't have a lot of friends. Outwardly, his life could have suggested reasons for distress, but his inner life was completely grounded in the obvious truth of things. He not only witnessed "it all," but paradoxically, lived as the obvious truth of "Just This." He was both the witnesser and the witness, identical to both dynamics simultaneously!

Lee's life proceeded in quite an ordinary way until he discovered the human potential movement in 1970. As with every new interest, he threw himself into it completely (another interesting period of five years prior to that was completely comsumed by popular dancing!). Lee attended an introduction to one of the schools of "human potential", showed an immediate grasp of the principles, dropped out of graduate school, became a teacher within the school, then a director, and soon saw its limitations. This time he had transcended not just the specific subject, which interestingly enough was the mind, but the limitation of *any* mere experience.

Lee's most famous quote is, "Enlightenment is the knowledge that all experience is transitory, including enlightenment." After the initial burst of energy of reentry into his Divine destiny, Lee soon saw that enlightenment is not supported—not by the ones who loved and supported him, and certainly not by the world. He had seen his work as that of awakening others but it was not going to be as easy as he had thought! He saw the necessity of a culture to sustain enlightenment and it didn't exist. He would have to create this culture with those around him and set about to do just this, manifesting a certain genius in recognizing the potential of the *seemingly* very ordinary people who were attracted to him. They weren't the famous, or rich, or very successful, but they were filled with the light of Lee's vision, and connected to His Heart with the disciplines of Love and Devotion. Lee often talks about how the core group comes from the "streets" and how there is no substitute for "street wisdom." They were ready to do this work and the "streets" taught them the abilities necessary to begin and to persevere. So, with these few, he began the experiment.

The experiment is now nine years old and we finally feel ready to describe this Work and what it means. This introduction will be an attempt to describe clearly the workings of the Godman, his Offering, Teaching and relationship with students. It is also the description of a true spiritual culture in the making and what this means for mankind as its existence on earth becomes more and more tenuous. We want to communicate the urgency to submit to this Way and the joy of it. Lee has described our natural condition as the Primacy of Natural Ecstasy and this is our destiny in His Company. He recently spoke to the core group:

"In the last eight years, you have generated experientially, as a community, a spiritual culture and the expansive realms of experience that embrace and validate every single written teaching document that has been published today, from every ancient spiritual tradition. We have built up a tremendous spiritual culture, full of incredible power, but we haven't been real students.

"Unfortunately, you haven't consistently recorded and recognized what is meant by your work. We haven't been able to communicate that, except in a personal way. You are examples within the confines of your own personal dynamic, but don't radiate your sanctity and the vision of this Work and this School to others as effectively as you should.

"What we're doing here now is putting that experience in perspective, so that even you who have created and generated it, recognize what it is you have done. That is what makes the Teaching available."

Lee said this to us just months ago, yet the Hohm Community has been engaging the long and difficult aim of establishing a culture that would sustain enlightenment for quite some time. He told us that we were already enlightened, that there was nothing to "attain", but it became quite clear from the beginning of the community that people weren't living an enlightened life. We were disposed to a worldly, self-indulgent lifestyle and attempted to superimpose a few spiritual disciplines and a bit of nondualistic philosophy on top of that. It obviously couldn't work that way. We needed to *be* different, not just pretend differences with no True shift of context. We needed to be *disposed* to an Enlightened life, which is already true of us, not simply make our spiritual lives an academic exercise, embellished by a few muscled disciplines.

Lee has described the context of our existence as Organic Innocence. It is the very ground of being out of which the body arises, or in other words, it is the divine matrix of individuated consciousness. It is called Organic because we are organic, chemical, biological beings, and it is Innocent because of the nature of already present Enlightenment. We *are* the Primacy of God, we needn't attain it, and the Primacy of God is, after all, Innocent. "Organic Innocence, this specific language, couldn't be used for the context of all manifestation, but for the *particular* context of organic manifestation, and that's important because organic manifestion has more of a defined leeway in terms of will, intention, free choice and all of those things that philosophers love to discuss."

If we had never resorted to identification with self-reference, this context would have determined our maturation as human beings and expressed itself in the Primacy of Natural Ecstasy. But, from the earliest age we perceived distinction between ourselves and others and the immediate result of this is the urge to protect the 'self' from extinction.

Given the proper education (which we are attempting to do in our culture), there would not remain the identification with ego as if ego were separate from or even antagonistic to the Divine Reality or God. It would be seen simply as a function of the organism—a very necessary function of the organism, but not the master of it.

The Primacy of Natural Ecstasy is the actual recognizable manifestation of Organic Innocence, the personification of it in individuation, or the point prior to self reference. This condition is inherent in our organism. It is the natural expression of our humanity in its Innocence. It is THE primary mood of our essence as conscious beings. It is ecstatic in the original sense of the word—to stand outside of oneself, outside of our usual identification with ego, free of the analytical or reflective dichotomies that are a result of the activity of ego. Softness, vulnerability, spontaneity, kindness, goodness, compassion, real pride, dignity, are inherent in our natural, primary condition, in the Primacy of God as man. All things are simply obvious, and what is required arises as perfect knowing. "To rest in the Primacy of Natural Ecstasy is to function purely out of the natural response of essence to circumstance, to function rawly, organically, intuitively, with no analytical or critical interference."

So, what part does the Godman play in this? It is very common in 'New Age' consciousness for individuals to think that they can surrender to the Will of God without help, or to assume all manifestation can be an ultimate "teacher." And even if this were possible, what better opportunity to test one's 'enlightenment' could there be than to be in the company of the Godman? Japanese Zen Masters were famous for 'testing' their enlightenment in the company of those they recognized to have realized permanent *satori*[1]. And often, they found themselves limited in their understanding and remained as students until their teachers were satisfied and sent them away. They knew that ego is dangerously clever—it can do a rather good imitation of an enlightened condition and will provide the circumstances to protect such an imitation. We can too easily kid ourselves, too easily insulate ourselves from real relationship. Or we can simply have a very limited and naive view of what an enlightened disposition is, based not on Real Education but on our own personal opinions and colored by our own neuroses. In this case education can be enough to expose misunderstanding to the light of objective clarity.

The Godman is identical to the Great Process of Divine Evolution. And as the Great Process, his very presence demands that *all* aspects

[1]Satori is the state of absolute clarity as expressed in the Zen tradition beginning in a momentary experience and eventually culminating in the total unity of "ordinary" consciousness with enlightened mind, or Buddha mind.

of that Process conform to its inclusive movement. The Godman provides for those in His company, the dynamic necessary to urge this alignment.The universe in all its many forms is not a static or chaotic event. Meher Baba[2] has described in great detail the evolution of God becoming matter and evolving back to God. God never changes, but nevertheless the Great Process of Divine Evolution embraces the whole dynamic of leaps in evolution, leaps in consciousness. We can submit to it, becoming slaves to the Will of God, or, because we can identify with an illusory, though convincing sense of separate consciousness, we can resist the Process. We do not evolve to enlightenment, rather, the Great Process of Divine Evolution occurs whether we are responsible for our "own" enlightenment or not. We "evolve" in spite of our "selves" or we "evolve" with conscious participation through submission.

This ever present demand to align oneself with God's Will and the actual movement in consciousness to do that, is what Lee refers to as Divine Influence. It is not an influence in the sense of an emanation or a power, it is simply the expectation made by the form of the Godman for one to assume the truth of things. "Divine Influence is, to put it in human terms, the genetic demand to be what you have been created to be, ultimately. It is the demand to be, as a human being, completely submitted to the Great Process of Divine Evolution in the mood of the Primacy of Natural Ecstasy, and it is the actual capacity to do so."

Many lesser teachers have mistaken the current of life-force in the body, often called *shakti,* to be divinely influential, to be enough to move people out of identification into submission to the Will of God. The teacher intentionally intensifies this energy in the student so that it may move through the body and various chakras.[3] The idea is that if one submits oneself to this energy, it will be enough to purify and realign one with God's Will.

But Shakti is much more than mere energy play in the body. Shakti is all of manifestation and in its ultimate expression for humans, Shakti *is* the Primacy of Natural Ecstasy. Organic Innocence is Shiva[4], it is a potential defined by pure consciousness and its ultimate possible ex-

[2]Meher Baba is a renowned 20th century Indian spiritual Master who offered his students a life of love and sacrifice—never using miracles or spectacular effects in his work with them.

[3]Subtle energy centers in the body traditionally associated with either a major nerve plexus or gland, at seven significant points of the bodily structure.

[4]Shiva is the male dynamic, the essence of consciousness itself, the intelligence of creation, and Shakti (traditional portrayed as Shiva's consort in traditional Indian mythology) is the female dynamic, the material of creation, the energy and movement of all form and life. Shiva is knowledge and Shakti is action, or Shiva's knowledge put into being and practice.

pression and the Primacy of Natural Ecstasy is the manifestation of that personified potential. Shakti is the Great Process of Divine Evolution manifesting in the mood of the Primacy of Natural Ecstasy.

The Great Process of Divine Evolution can also be described as the inclusive dynamic of all existence, manifest or nonmanifest. It defines the Will of God in the way humans can relate to it. The Will of God cannot be fixed to any particular movement, attitude, behavior, rule, assumption, etc.; it is defined in every moment. But the Great Process of Divine Evolution does define a movement inherent in us as human beings. There is a movement in the human being that includes the maturation of functions, the nervous system, the definition of specific abilities and roles.

Lee is all that he embraces, he intuitively recognizes the Will of God in every case, and he will move us to our own alignment with the Will of God through Divine Influence. Our resistance can be observed as ridiculous in the perception of the movement of universal creation. Everything dies and is devoured in its completely subsuming path.

"Everything is food for everything else." This law, the Law of Sacrifice, is the underlying principle of divine evolutionary creation. It is the matrix of relationship and submission expresses itself in the Primacy of Natural Ecstasy. We are creatures who have chosen suffering over our God-given destiny and the Godman reminds us of our choice in every moment. His presence is communion, his condition of Organic Innocence speaks to our condition of Organic Innocence. He is the critical interface of what is already true and all the conditioning which isolates us from what is true. And this relationship is the foundation of our realignment to the Great Process.

But we do lack the education to make use of this relationship optimally so Lee has also served the function of Teacher, being a source of Wisdom and Education. This is his aspect that provides the knowledge and milieu in which alignment can take place. A Godman does not always function as Teacher, not even necessarily as spiritual Master. The Godman may never take students, so it is the spiritual Master who engages devotees in order to awaken them. We need to understand how a Master works, in particular, how Lee works, since he brings his own uniqueness to this timeless play.

Some spiritual Masters work from above, pulling their students up, some Masters place themselves below and push their students up—Lee's way has been to meet his students at their own level, although he can easefully push from below (with rakishness and flair) or gracefully pull from above (with Elegance and sophistication) when that is what any given circumstance demands. Early in 1977, Lee saw that he would have to engage his students at their level of psychological need before they could begin 'spiritual' work. Certainly there was a willingness on the part of students to begin 'real work', but we are so insecure as men and women, so ill equipped to begin 'real work', that even the most basic demands of simple discipline and criticism are often beyond our capacity when we first approach the Teacher. Lee's response to this need was to sacrifice his own free manifestation while maintaining his enlightened disposition. He has told us many times, "My hands are tied. I am bound to you and I am only Free to give you more to the degree that you are free to accept what I already offer." The spiritual Master had submitted himself to his close students completely and his way of working with them reflected this. Lee has quoted Shirdi Sai Baba many times in reference to this, "I give you what you want until you begin to want what I want to give you." Shirdi Sai Baba was a Godman who lived in Shirdi, India in the 19th and early 20th century with whom Lee has a special affinity. In fact, students of Lee have often felt his presence or even seen him to be Shirdi Sai Baba in the setting of the Darshan Hall and at other sacred spots. Every true Teacher subsumes every previous Teacher's expression, so it is quite common for Teachers to literally communicate the actual presence of other teachers, dead and alive. Particular lineages have sympathies to certain teachers because of cultural and spiritual communications, in Lee's case, it has been most common for him to express those of Shirdi Sai Baba, Ramana Maharshi, Ram Surat Kumar, Meher Baba, Nityananda and Krishna. But there have been periods in the history of the community when he has expressed such vastly different communications as the Zen lineages, offering koans to students, mystical brotherhoods of Sufism, Jesus, and Buddha. During our Guru Purnima celebration of 1979, Lee literally became all of these Teachers, one after another, during Darshan, revealing his perfect communication as the Godman. Students recognized all these different Teachers in both visionary and ordinary states of consciousness, and naturally felt particular personal affinities, those with an affinity to Buddhism literally saw the Buddha, others who yearned for Krishna, saw him as Krishna, and heard Krishna's flute (driven to frenzies of ecstacy as were the gopis).

The spiritual Master must be free to manifest (not merely imitate) *whatever* is required to awaken his students. Sometimes this activity simply mirrors student's cramps, appearing offensive, immoral, or even just ordinary. Lee's admonition again echoing the Divine Speech of past Godmen, is, "Do as I say, not as I do" and even though this could mean outrageous behavior to the casual observer, in Lee's particular case, it has tended to be perfectly ordinary in form. Lee is Master of ordinariness—he has appeared so ordinary, so much like us at times that he has made it impossible for us to adopt a particular posture or form of behavior as enlightened. His ordinariness has the effect of throwing us back to our own understanding, disallowing dogmatism, lack of humor and rigid or righteous indignations. It may only be the twinkle in his eye that lets us know he is imitating us at times, but that twinkle has been there even when he has appeared to be in a rage. As ordinary as he appears, he never lets us forget his transcendental delight.

The spiritual Master responds completely to us, is completely vulnerable to us and this meeting is the meeting of lovers. The spiritual Master is bound to us through love and only in our love for him can we trust him to see us through this process. His love creates vulnerability in us, often embarrasses us—it is a little frightening so we would rather think we had been tricked or seduced. And over time a tension is created, because we have expectations of how love is supposed to be and this love doesn't meet with those expectations. Lee's love doesn't pamper or coddle, "Compassion is in response to need not expectancy." It is completely uncompromising, and the more maturity Lee sees in his students, the less pleased he is with the remaining resistance and vital recoil.

Love is spoken about so casually today that I'm reluctant to even use the word. Almost any kind of emotional titillation is called love and it's obvious that that kind of love can't be trusted. Love is real only when the one who loves has nothing to lose. This kind of love is a rare treasure amongst men and the recognition of the spiritual Master's love is one of the first things that draws us to him. Nothing but love can make the path of becoming selfless, becoming a Slave to the Will of God, worth the struggle. Lee, when a teacher of a popular positive thinking methodology, lived a life of constant bubbly, gleeful happiness and was in great social demand, but his acquaintances proved as fleeting and fickle as if he were dull and uninspiring. Now, although his demeanor shifts as rapidly as the sand in a desert windstorm, though, like us, he is often (is he or does he merely appear so?) angry, annoyed, petty, his essence is Wisdom, and unlike his previous sugary "face", this less attractive face is embraced by friends who love him as they do themselves (and more so at times), with a dedication and consistency unusual anywhere. We are bound in our selfishness and self-importance, we have a hundred strategies for self protection—we do not surrender easily. We can want truth with great will and intensity, but this process is made humanly possible through love (whatever we think that to be—our understanding will mature in time.)

This has been a hard path, because our school has not functioned with rules and regulations to enforce practices or behavior. It has been left to the individual to develop conscience in relationship to his work. True, Divine Influence is always moving us in this direction, and peer pressure is a factor, but it is more common in spiritual schools for the Teacher or the school itself to enforce the "proper" alignment. In this school, the alignment of the group to the disposition of enlightenment has determined the culture. Lee has refused to let the maturity of a few determine the form, only to have it pulled down by the immaturity of the group. The emphasis has always been on establishing an enlightened culture, of determining the strength of the group from its weakest link.

Essentially, there is nothing to be attained. We do mature in various stages of alignment, but we either live from the disposition of enlightenment, or we don't. This understanding has been encouraged in several ways. One way is that Lee does not make much of students' breakthroughs. "Whaddaya want, a medal?" is Lee's retort when a student expects to be "recognized" (read lauded and substantiated as a being for what should be already and *always* perfectly true of one anyway) for some movement of clarity or freedom. Not that they aren't recognized, but consistency is determined over time. "Time is the Great Tester," is Lee's humorous and regular admonition. His mode of teaching has been to nurture rather than to test, to push limits with patience and encouragement, always waiting for his students to shift movement into higher levels of alignment. We are asked to come to know what is real through our own recognition, to bring our own strength and understanding to this process. He waits for us to mature, not testing in dramatic ways that disrupt the environment. He waits as a beggar, 'giving in so as to conquer,' (the essential "law" of the art of Judo.) His lineage is that of Beggar Kings, his own Master living as a beggar, dressed in rags, but with the undeniable presence and elegance of the most Regal Monarch. This subtle, and quiet way has allowed students to come together and support one another in an exceptional way, testing and maturing them in patience and humility. Our expression too must become that of a True beggar—humble, quiet, sensitive.

Most of the ways Lee works with us are very subtle. Great sensitivity is required on the part of the student to make use of what is offered. Lee's way is to hint, both by action and speech, rather than to give linear explanations to the mind. As the Godman, his communications are Divinely Influential, they are exactly what is required in every circumstance, but we are certainly not trained to see this. When we question, we must first know what we are asking, (and if we don't Lee may answer us in a way that we don't recognize because he is answering what we are 'really' asking), we need to be able to listen to what he is telling us, (most of us don't even hear what is being said accurately), and then we need to be able to accept and use the answer. At this stage, when we don't receive the answer that we wanted, we often argue with what Lee has said. He tells us, "My first suggestion is what I mean, if you don't take it, I'll agree with you." And then, to actually act on what he has told us, if and when we understand it, requires great integrity. It is not enough to understand—we must act on what we know. This is literally what is meant by the statement that we are already enlightened but we are not living an enlightened life.

A young man came to our school very eager to begin spiritual work. He was given a living and working situation that wasn't as comfortable as he liked, but he was willing to put up with them because he was here to do spiritual work. But the Master didn't speak to him often or confront him with his cramps, which he knew must be there. He became more and more frustrated with his work and living companions and wondered when the Master would begin to work with him. One day, when speaking with a senior student, he expressed his frustration. He was reminded that one of the ways the Master works is simply to provide the perfect circumstances for each individual in which to observe himself, his resistances, etc. The living environment into which this student was thrown were perfect to reveal to him what he needed to work on. The spiritual Master didn't have to confront him or set up an artificial circumstance to show him what he needed to see, but he did have to learn where to look. We have to learn to make use of whatever is present and use that for our work. What is present here, under Lee's Divine Influence is *precisely* for us, there is no randomness to what arises.

In the Disposition of Enlightenment, the essence of everything is tacitly recognized and responded to from a like space. It is not a matter of being untouched by reality, but rather, being completely and passionately involved, free to respond however circumstances require. Everything is recognized as unique but not separate from God, distinct in its own right, but not distinct from the Matrix of Divine Inclusiveness. So, as we mature in our alignment to the disposition of enlightenment, the more obvious our own particular qualities become and each of us begins to manifest who we really are—"I don't want anyone's Awakening to be a mimic of me," Lee says, reminding us to be that which we are, not a copy of someone else, even the Master, though when we are ourselves, we cannot help but realize that the Master IS us, in a literal way.

Lee has trained us to draw principle from from every source available, to make use of whatever is present, rather than simply adopting his own particular criticisms or leanings towards certain sources. He makes teaching lessons from such diverse sources as Bob Dylan, Nijinsky, Rita Mae Brown, even his dog, and so a musician learns how he can draw principle from music, a dancer from dance, a carpenter from his work. The world and its delusions are also harshly criticized as to the "worldly" motivation, or assumption of suffering, not for its essential, already true Reality or Enlightenment. His work with us has been designed to give us a balance between the critical view of 'the world' and how to extract truth from anything and everything. His emphasis is on realizing the *context* of an Enlightened disposition, thereby making all things available to use, rather than attempting, an impossible task by his confession, to somehow "spiritualize" the world's content. Texture, not form, is where he directs our focus. Personally, Lee never loses touch with "the streets" and this has given a rare quality to the Hohm Community. When the Master talks about "going slumming," he could mean going to the local dance joint, attending a cello concert, playing in a local softball game, or visiting the latest high society art flash. There is a tone of honor and respect for human beings, for other schools and other teachers; what is of value is used, what isn't is discarded. Arrogance as individuals and as a school is strongly criticized. Even Pavarotti, the great Italian tenor has said that he can learn something from almost any singer, because every singer can do one thing better. This is an attitude to be embraced!

The Master's way of working with us over the years has been to reveal to us first what isn't aligned to the Great Process of Divine Evolution—our recoil, psychological cramps, our fear, anger, and self importance; and to shine light on what is real and true, what makes for an enlightened culture.

But Lee has offered us more than the inevitable realization of our enlightenment in His company. He offers a consideration of God as Beloved that has been described historically only from the limited perspective of separation from God. Utterly unique in Lee's Teaching is the consideration of the non-dualistic realization of our always present enlightenment *with* the vision of God as Personal, as the Beloved of Lovers of God. Is God Personal? Does God have form? Is God simply what is, without separation from anything? Is God consciousness, what is prior to manifestation? These vastly different revelations seem to be so opposed to one another that for thousands of years mankind has vainly argued over them, insisting that one or the other realization was incomplete. Lee's answer is yes—God is the Great Process of Divine Evolution, that there is nothing, absolutely no-thing other than God, and, at the same time, for human beings, the greatest Gift, in fact, the *only* Gift, is the vision of God in personal form, all else being already presently True and nondualistic Reality. *The Only Grace is Loving God* is Lee's definitive statement of this remarkable perspective. His message should be considered by scholars and students alike as a radical departure from traditional and contemporary teachings, even those of radical teachers. In the light of Lee's undeniable manifestation as an 'unordinary' human being, his startling consideration of Gift, Grace, Beloved, the Will of God and the Whim of God can't be swept under the table if we are at all willing to have our comfortable opinions (and they can only be opinions) shaken. What does an 'enlightened' Man have to say about God as a-lawful, as The Personal God who is Whimsical, who's expression is pure Caprice, outside of the Law of the Great Process of Divine Evolution? This is a subject that is rarely, if ever, touched even by the most serious of spiritual students.

The spiritual Master has said, "(my) contribution to True *Human* Culture is the Gospel that the *only* Grace is Loving God. That as human beings we *must* be submitted to the Law and that we *may* be submitted to the delight and majesty that is God's Whimsical shower of Grace, his *only* Grace, Loving Him."[1]

This profound message is not a mere philosophical argument. It has implications so far-reaching for us as human beings, that to ignore it is to ignore our 'greatest possibility.' "Loving God is the epitome, the Holy acme of human possibility, not the culmination of endless incarnations leading up to the knowledge of and existence as the Truth of God in the form of His Being as the Great Process of Divine Evolution. The highest destiny and only evolutionary perfection of man is Awakening, the highest possibility of man is Loving God. Loving God is Gift, the *only* Grace there is."[2]

This is a rare Gift not bestowed often on human beings. Lovers of God are rarer than those sent to awaken man through Divine Influence. So what does Lee mean by "Loving God?" What does it matter to us that anyone should Love God? Why does he offer us the Consideration of Loving God? What are the implications of such a confusing statement?

Very, very briefly—Lee speaks of Loving God as a condition, given in Whimsy "in which the entire Radiance or expression of universal Light, impersonally breathed in every moment and to everyone/everything, is limited to one channel or beam of direction which is God in Personal Form."[3] Loving God is not what the usual man thinks or assumes. It is not the warm, cozy, comfortable emotionality that usually passes for love. It isn't the feeling of tenderness towards an "all-caring" father-figure-God. It is not light and airy, it is consuming and overwhelming, blinding to all but the Beloved. When one is Awake, one *is* Love, radiant in all directions. One who Loves God is completely absorbed in God as the Beloved. This vision could not be sustained by one still under the illusion of separation from God. Only one already aligned to the Great Process of Divine Evolution, already surrendered to the Will of God can make the leap of viewing God as separate. It would be too agonizing for ego to bear the vision of Personal God always apart, because its motivation is survival. Loving God as presented conventionally sounds very nice, homey, kind of a good feeling inside. If we were to truly be Gifted with God as Whimsical, completely outside of the Law of our existence as human beings, it would be terrifying to us. "The Lover of God has been reborn out of union, reborn into separation once again, but not to suffer as the common man but in order to Love God from that separateness."[4]

[1]Lee Lozowick, *The Only Grace is Loving God*, (Hohm Press), p. 25.
[2]Lozowick, p. 72.
[3]Lozowick, p. 3.
[4]Lozowick, p. 78.

The very idea "shatters the intuition of the safety and security of an Awakened life of non-dualism and Realized perspective."[5] The Consideration of Loving God humbles us, creating "a very necessary vulnerability which makes the culture of one's relationship to God warm, available, and deeply respectful...The real feeling for Loving God will undermine any complacency, will totally destroy any security that one has invested in things that are inherently false or illusory. Loving God, the deep consideration of this idea of the Whim of God as the *only* Grace there is, will shatter any egoistic belief systems about Enlightenment, God, or Awakened life that one has surrounded oneself with. Not only will complacency be shattered but the possibility of Loving God will not only be entertained in a serious way but will be related to in a context that brings respect, awe, gratitude, and a sort of ever present excitement to every moment of one's spiritual involvement."[6]

And what about the one Gifted with Loving God? He is lost in his vision of the Beloved, blind to the mediocrity of anything else. And for the rest of us—he is our salvation. One who has become God, who is Slave to the Will of God cannot petition God. "The Awakened one has become God. The Lover of God has returned to his humanity..."[7] He makes our continuing existence as human beings more than just a random event. He has been Gifted with a personal relationship with God and God hears him. Were it not possible for man to Love God, there would be only an arbitrary reason for our existence. That we can be personally noticed by God is perhaps the greatest implication of the existence of Lovers of God. They are our humanity.

This consideration has profound import to the culture we have been creating under Lee's guidance. It demands the highest of human life, one full of reverence, gratitude, awe, surrender, compassion, kindness. Because the *only* Gift is Loving God, there is nothing "special" about enlightenment—it is obvious and humbling to act in accordance with what we know.

"Saqi" is the name that has arisen for Lee in his offering of the Consideration of Loving God. It is a traditional reference for one's Teacher in the Sufi tradition and means literally, the wine pourer, the Tavern boy. We use it for Lee in his context as the one who intoxicates, the one who pours the wine of the Beloved for his friends. It is a name to be used when we feel the sweetness of our relationship to him rather than the name to honour him as spiritual Master.

The name given Lee that encompasses both his function of spiritual

[5]Lee Lozowick, *The Only Grace is Loving God,* p. 79.
[6]Lee Lozowick, pgs. 79-80.
[7]Lee Lozowick, p. 75.

Master and Saqi is "EliRam," My God, the Highest. It is a name of God, an invocation of God, and glorifies the highest realization of Man. EliRam is the sacred and holy name of our Master, communicating his perfect and complete Realization and Offering. It is the name to remember God in the Form of the One Who lives amongst us.

We have chosen to use the name Lee when referring to our spiritual Master in *Living God Blues*, because of the particular flavour of this book.

An enlightened culture means that we gather together with one another as devotees, not that we come to gain our own personal enlightenment and then move on to become teachers on our own. A truly enlightened culture is one free of petty self-referencing, one full of the effacement of the individual in the joy of service and devotion to God. A spiritual Master gathers his own together and they remain devotees in this play. Very rarely, if ever, would someone be sent out by the Master to establish a school of his own, except in the context of the communication of the teaching through outreach work. People visit Lee, often experience a minor satori, a little blip of ecstacy, then go off as if they were now his equal. It is more common than might be imagined, and should be a profound lesson for those who are serious about realizing the Primacy of Natural Ecstasy. It takes many individuals and a great deal of time, several generations, ideally, to firmly establish a human culture, a culture in which *all* areas of human endeavor are aligned with the context of Organic Innocence rather than the context of identification with survival, and we have had to start from scratch. Everything from pregnancy, childbirth and child raising to food, the arts, right livelihood, politics, and education is lived, not from the standpoint of attainment, but as the proper orientation, free of the petty, problematic disposition of egoic life. The mind, body and emotions are not in conflict with one another and life is full of joy in the good company of one another; people surrendered to God are surrendered to one another, fully able to serve one another, the community and God, however that manifests in each individual's case. This is a far cry from the competitiveness, moods of envy, adolescent criticism, revolutionary attitudes, cliquishness, obsession with war, violence, sex, and sports that make for most interaction in society.

People need help to shift their context from identification with the illusion of lack of Being or enlightenment, to that of Organic Innocence, and the spiritual Master along with the true culture provide that help. Each individual spontaneously moves through alignment of higher levels of life (the nervous system transfiguration and all its attendant dynamics, mystical and otherwise) and the culture accomodates periods of absorption or ecstatic manifestation. In time, the culture itself would assume the function of the spiritual Master as senior men and women would be considered the source of wisdom along with empowered practices, prayers, shrines etc. And in a very far-reaching way, the sacred objects and objective art created in such a culture would survive as a time capsule of what is highest in man, through the darkness of the Kali yuga.[1]

One of the most important ways of establishing this is in the education of children. It is especially important that children be educated from birth into the disposition of enlightenment and learn discrimination as to what is Real. We will never remain completely apart from society at large, so it is crucial that discernment, rather than dogmatism, be established in children. This can't happen unless children come to trust themselves—we all suffer from pernicious insecurity and doubt in our own worth as human beings. This would not happen to children brought up sensitively, with discipline and humour and a recognition of the essence of the child. Child raising is one of the most important areas of our consideration. Children should ideally be immersed in a culture fully cognizant of a tacit Realization of inclusive Divine Reality, a culture completely grounded in already present enlightenment.

An enlightened culture is elegant in all of its manifestations. How we walk, dress, talk, interact with friends and lovers, create our environments, establish a natural protocol—all of these things easefully and spontaneously become simple and clean. There is a natural respect for spaces, children, senior students, men and a men's culture, women and a women's culture, and the spiritual Master. As we mature in our submission to this Way, our body's sensitivity informs us of dissonance with the environment so that we can correct it and the disposition of Elegance manifests as a relaxed and delightful camaraderie, free of the ordinary tensions and competitiveness inherent in conventional social gatherings in which everyone is trying to survive over and against everyone else.

The whole New Age concept of freedom is a concept of a childish, anarchic rebellion against Holy Authority and True Wisdom. In a real culture there is a natural and elegant protocol, free of tension and recoil. It is not Lee's way to bend people to the rules of arbitrary discipline;

[1]The Kali yuga, according to Vedic scriptures is the current dark age of history begun five thousand years ago and continuing for a further 427,000 years. It precedes the Golden Age.

elegant protocol is expected to arise out of a mature approach (when one is submitted to the Way, if one acts in a way that is dissonant, it will be felt immediately in the body and can be corrected.) Until this maturity is evident, the rules that do exist should be viewed as having arisen to help us turn our attention where we have not been trained. The rules of basic manners and etiquette should be observed, exceptions should be given not taken and there should be a natural respect and timidness in relationship to new environments.

The American is famous for his insensitivity and lack of respect for other cultures and even in his own culture has not been properly educated to approach sacred or holy spaces. He has also shown an heroic and energetic movement to desecrate any spaces with any grain of sanctity—for example, the desecration of national parks and monuments. On Lee's first trip to India with several devotees (three months after Hohm's inception), one of the men yodelled as loud as he could in the Taj Mahal (despite posted signs all over requesting silence), ostensibly to "test the echo dynamics" but obviously to glaringly echo his own ego. He was just being the "ugly American" of recent fable. This event, amongst an almost unending stream of grossly inappropriate activity, was among the deciding factors for Lee to finish the last two thirds of the trip with his two women devotees, sending the men back to New Jersey, and sparking a now famous teaching lesson.

So we should assume ignorance and humility until we are able to embrace a certain level of education and responsible activity in relationship to that education.

As informal as our School appears to be, the informality is not a function of casualness, but a function of the communion with the Divine source of Light—the spiritual Master.

This is a very great undertaking. It takes extraordinary strength, devotion, sacrifice and love on the part of the student of this Way, and the spiritual Master (who has no choice in the matter!) It begins with submission to the Way offered by the spiritual Master and entails a life of discipline and integrity. When you have found your Teacher, you have essentially finished seeking and can begin becoming responsible for the understanding that brought you to the Teacher. This means we begin by taking up the conditions of practice as outlined by Lee. It is a common illusion that freedom is not having to do anything we don't want to. To ego, of course, there is no freedom possible because it is locked into a "do or die" dynamic of inflexible posturing and behavioral manifestation. Part of its "game" is to pretend freedom is possible, to seek it, and to ostensibly attain it in order to fool the "being" into thinking it need not continue to attempt transcendence, as the context of

Organic Innocence is always demanding through instinct and intuition. Ego's game is to *imply* freedom by the refusal to follow any rules, to function however one feels like in the moment (the feeling, of course, being designed and controlled absolutely by ego itself!). It designs the perfect antagonism to Real Freedom. The real devotee finds freedom in the same routine, adopting the conditions of the spiritual Master as the natural and appropriate way of aligning oneself to the Great Process of Divine Evolution in his Company.

The Teaching is essentially a description of the cramp, the delusion of who we think we are, of what *is* actually true in every moment, and the means of living and realizing the truth from the Disposition of Enlightenment. Lee has given us several practices that work with each of these different areas. Each of them changes as we mature in our understanding, Lee offering specific forms of their use to students in His company. He allows us to work with each practice in our own way, and when discipline and the great tester 'time' have matured our personal use of these recommendations, Lee will give us the exact instruction necessary to rest in the appropriate disposition of practice.

So here we will simply describe the principles of each of these practices, recommending that their optimal use is only made in complete submission to this Way. When given, they are used randomly and spontaneously in relationship to what arises, with whatever insight and maturity is present for us.

Reactional Enquiry is used to examine the cramp, to Pay Attention, and Assertion 'asserts' what is true. It *is* Remembrance.

Reactional Enquiry is the phrase, "Who am I kidding?"[1] It is the humorous enquiry of what we are up to in every moment, and is quite unlike the heavy, serious, solemn attitude most people expect of religious or spiritual practices. It is meant in all seriousness, but cuts the habitual mood of our context of isolation. When it is given to us as a practice, we begin to use it with intention, but over time it arises spontaneously as a mood that obviates the cramp of ego. "Who am I kidding?" communicates the characteristic delight and playfulness of Lee's disposition. How can we maintain the illusion we have always assumed to be real if we engage Reactional Enquiry with sincerity?

Enquiry can and should be used to examine all our reactions, motiva-

[1]Lee Lozowick, *Laughter of the Stones,* The Divine Road of Reactional Enquiry, (Hohm Press), pgs. 65-68.

tions, impulses, urges, considerations, opinions, etc. until our inspection of ourselves deepens into the roots of these manifestations. The practice "eventually yields its falseness and superficiality to what is True and Real. The True and/or Real is always hidden within the false but is so obvious that it is never seen until the very last moment. It is so obvious, in fact, that it seems too simple and too pure to be true and since humans don't want to ever be "wrong" (not that they're ever right) they look right past the obviousness (they don't want to be simplistic either so they ignore anything that's too simple) and try to figure out an intricate and highly sophisticated truth in the illusion, thereby only causing untold problems and confusion."[2]

The foundation for both Reactional Enquiry and Assertion is Paying Attention and Remembering, the simple observation of things prior to the need to react to them. We must notice what is arising with consciousness and remember what is prior in understanding before we can enquire of it. So, essentially this process consists of seeing what one is up to, or purification through Paying Attention and Reactional Enquiry in conjunction with the conditions; Remembering, in its principle stage ("there is nothing to be attained"); and fully expressing our manifestation as human beings through Assertion, or Remembering in its ultimate expression.

Assertion is Lee's individualized practice (although calling it a practice is really a convenience of language), that embodies both the context of Organic Innocence and the Great Process of Divine Evolution. It is the Tacit Recognition of already present Enlightenment, asserting what is already True in every moment, without any assumption of the need to change circumstance, belief or attitude, and manifesting as free movement. Everything is simply and obviously what it is, in the Primacy of Natural Ecstasy.

But there still remains the paradox of embodiment (Shakti), seemingly separate and isolated. The consequence of "just this" in the appropriate realization, obviates this dilemma and the subjectivity implied by "this." The traditional Indian practice of referring to God as "That" is obviously a fallacy of perception because "That" implies distance and temporality, that God is "other," whereas "this", realized, *is* "just this."

These "practices" are really not new creations that we learn to superimpose on our lives. Paying Attention and Remembering is the natural and primary movement of consciousness—consciousness remembering consciousness, whether we participate in its arising or not. We need only align ourselves with this eternal and ever-present process,

[2]Lee Lozowick, *Laughter of the Stones*, (Hohm Press), p. 66.

and in doing so we consciously participate as Assertion. Our very existence is the mysterious and 'magical' consequence of Assertion and its mood expresses itself in the Primacy of Natural Ecstasy. "Just this" evokes awe, delight, gratitude, reverence, and as such is the ground for an enlightened, elegant, juicy, rich, passionate and thoroughly enjoyable life.

The conditions given to us by Lee are similar to that of any Real school and include certain practices. But because they have been offered specifically by Lee, they embody his Influence, making them different in context from any self-chosen forms of discipline.

We are asked to stop smoking, drinking, and taking drugs. We adopt a sane and life enhancing lacto-vegetarian diet and begin to exercise and meditate daily. We are asked to work at a responsible job, and tithe out of our income from that job to the support of the community. A list of Hohm's literature and traditional spiritual and classical literature is given us for study. We also maintain a monogamous sexual relationship, and perhaps live in a community household. In all of this, we tend to have a vague conception of the purpose of the requirements, usually mistaking their ego-motivated fulfillment as an indication that we are living spiritual life. We are simply taking on the form of an appropriate, functional life as Lee stipulates and over time, as we begin to *do* the practices, not just fulfill a specific form, we realize the truth of them. In the process of willfully fulfilling the requirements, the fact that we fundamentally resist an Enlightened life is clearly demonstrated to us. Even these basic functional aspects of life have to be forced at first, showing us our literal refusal of Happiness. "The conditions of sadhana must be understood clearly enough so that there is no neurotic dependency on those conditions and no righteous aura of discipline or 'holiness' surrounding them. The conditions are not to be lived for a certain period of time until they are transcended or no longer necessary, having achieved a particular end result. They are simply natural and appropriate aspects of our communion and friendship with our spiritual Master....The conditions are not even lifelong tasks or obligations. They can't really be fit into any spatial, temporal framework, even if the temporal framework is an eternal or permanent one over and against a mortal or temporary one. They are only the normal optimal processes of any Divinely moved human being."[1]

The conditions of practice as given by Lee are simple and ordinary. Many people approach our school having lived a life that included many or all of these elements. But they do not serve in the same way when practiced from the context of self-reference, and these people soon find that they are having difficulty in maintaining a discipline they thought established. Typically, the ordinary spiritual student, refusing the Sacrifice of the spiritual Master, employs disciplines in order to dominate or be superior, even though it may not look like it on the surface. Ego wants to be well-read, fit and attractive, mellow, strong and healthy and all of these things do arise in our practice of the conditions, as incidental effects. But more importantly, our practice of the conditions disposes us to surrender and the Remembrance of God and the spiritual Master.

This principle is why in traditional schools in which mantras are used, it is absolutely necessary for the mantra to be "given" directly by the Teacher, rather than just read in a book and practiced. It is the Teacher's essence infusing the communication that *is* the initiation, not the words alone. Because the conditions have been given by Lee, they *are* Him in essence, and our practice of them *is* the manifestation of alignment to the Will of God or enlightenment itself, not the means to eventual enlightenment.

Lee has said that if we do the conditions properly for a period of six months, we shouldn't have any neurotic questions to ask about ourselves, our practice, or our relationships. As we practice, we are literally aligning ourselves bodily to the Great Process of Divine Evolution, becoming more and more sensitive and open to the Divine Influence of the Godman and any situation we happen to be in. We come to spiritual life with great illusions—about who we are, about diet, about what is sacred, and something as simple as these disciplines can and will shake us from our narrow vision.

One should approach the conditions in the mood of surrender, devotion and obedience: in the mood of humor and gentleness, they can be felt, rather than mechanically performed. Understanding and sensitivity come from a feeling approach, not an aggressive or severe attitude towards discipline. The key to this approach is in the most primary of Lee's teaching tools—Paying Attention and Remembering.

Paying Attention is the simple observation of what arises, without analysis, compartmentalization and prejudice, recognizing, as an obvious fact of objective observation, that we are still motivated by cramps. In our clear view of what mechanically moves us, the tacit realization of the truth, Remembering, naturally arises. (It is Remember-

[1]Lee Lozowick, *The Yoga of Enlightenment/The Book of Unenlightenment,* (Hohm Press), p. 48

ing that brings us to the teaching in the first place—we recognize something we *already* know to be true.) Paying Attention is simply being conscious. It begins with an attentiveness to basic things like our body posture, tonal quality of voice and underneath, the subtle impulses that predispose these postures. We see habits, psychological strategies and in time we can begin to observe the primal cramp underlying them. The discipline of Paying Attention is what allows Remembering to establish us in the disposition of enlightenment.

We will discuss this further in the next section, but it is enough now to know that all the conditions should be practiced with as much attention as we are able to bring to them.

The most basic, and perhaps the most important of the conditions is study. It is recommended that we spend at least one to one and a half hours each day in serious study of the teaching. The foundation for study is our own literature, from which other literature, both traditional spiritual and classical literature, can be understood. Our books are necessary to familiarize ourselves with Lee's language and style of working and to ground us in the disposition of enlightenment. Study educates us to this process, literally feeding the mind, and keeps it focused on the Teaching, rather than lost in the quagmire of worldly distractions. The mind can be our greatest enemy or one of the greatest helps in keeping us established in this Way.

The Influence of Lee's Company gives people (if they are willing), a subconscious ability to discern anything approaching truth from things founded in illusory assumptions. When people study, one effect beyond any intellectual grasp of the material, is that they subconsciously learn to discern Elegance and spiritual truth from empty philosophy or self-important communications. The recommended reading list is specially chosen for the bodily communication the books make, and if we are submitted to Lee's Influence, we will get that communication whether it is conscious or not. The more we study, the more we become submitted to a life of happiness and submission to the Will of God.

The natural consequence of study is discernment—eventually we will read only that which is of value to our work, or is of pure delight! The study of traditional spiritual and classical literature greatly helps in learning discernment, if we approach it from the objective and critical context that our own literature can provide us with. Not all traditional spiritual literature is written from the disposition of enlightenment, but we can still make use of it if we know what level of maturity it applies to. Also, a different description of the same thing can evoke recognition, so the more descriptions we read, the more possibility there is for a deeper and broader understanding of the teaching. Study brings about

Remembering in both a quiet way and in a revelatory way and it is a common trap to think we've "got it" when we've just had a glorious revelation—it isn't worth very much if we still refuse to live what is revealed. Armchair devotees litter the field of self-illusion. Capturing the mind is one of ego's favorite ways of tricking us into thinking we understand. As a Chinese philosopher, Wang Yang-ming succinctly put it, "To know and not to act is not to know."

It is of value, too, to have an historical perspective on our teaching, to see not only that it is founded on great spiritual cultures, but that it subsumes all past accomplishments in its own present and most brilliant expression. This undermines self-importance (as if we were the only spiritual students the world has ever seen!) and also gives us a ground for communicating with students of other traditions. Even a lesser, or incomplete path, can be of value to someone who engages it with integrity. Lee has written a very serious sutra called "How not to Act Superior When You Really Are,"[1] that demolishes any incentive towards postures of false humility or supercilious arrogance.

The meditation we practice is a non-directed, simple observation of thoughts, emotions and bodily sensations as they arise, recognizing them as aspects of the non-exclusive whole. It illuminates our stream of consciousness, the limited and subjective realm we live in. No one thing, such as thoughts, is focused on—it is a common trap for people to assume that thoughts are more important than emotions or the body, so they become detached from thoughts in their meditation, but are instead captured by kundalini experiences or forms of emotional rapture. All things must be seen for what they are—some things have more value than others in relative terms, but not in the context of the Great Process of Divine Evolution. Over time more specific practices are given by Lee to mature students, but he is especially conservative in this regard, often waiting years before he gives them.

It is recommended that we sit every day for half an hour to one hour either at one sitting or morning and evening. Relaxed breathing, correct posture, a proper setting are all important but unlike many rigid meditations, when an itch or a buzzing of a fly interferes, Lee's advice is, "I recommend scratching."

Consistency in practice will make apparent a process within meditation over time, but as with most things, Lee doesn't give us the description of what will/should arise, but waits to confirm what we ourselves discover. It can be said that through meditation our misidentification with ego, and the things that define the context of survival, become

[1]Lee Lozowick, *Laughter of the Stones,* (Hohm Press), p. 109.

clarified so that the context of Organic Innocence can arise. We begin to see with much more objectivity and clarity and our internal wars begin to die down. The cycles we have discussed in the previous section also become clarified and the regularity with which we meditate determines how much of that objectivity we can carry with us throughout our day's activities.

When things become simply (or merely) obvious, we needn't maintain a willful or intentional disposition in relationship to equanimity, but our lives are "just" free and happy, not a knot of muscled yogas.

The condition of exercise completes the three most basic of the conditions. Like study and meditation, it must be done properly and with a feeling of Remembrance. Our exercise is designed to maintain a body that communicates the essence of Elegance, Elegance being the expression of Organic Innocence. It requires a body that is strong yet supple, vibrant and alive. Such a body is in a state of receptivity, optimally available and alert to the environment and Divine Influence. Secondarily, this requires that the body be purified, not only of toxins from this lifetime but also of karmic toxins that have been genetically and organically transmitted. Exercise practiced in the context of Paying Attention and Remembering does this as well.

We exercise for half an hour every day (women dividing this into twenty minutes of stretching and ten minutes of vigorous calisthenics and men dividing it into ten minutes of stretching and twenty minutes of vigorous exercise) and Lee recommends other activities such as yoga, martial arts, walking, swimming, classical dancing (modern jazz, aerobics have their place but *not* in the conditions), etc., be used as well. The form of exercise will change over time, hard styles moving into soft during certain periods and vice versa. After several years of practice, we will become vulnerable and intuitive to our own process, recognizing when random periods of change are necessary.

Besides these three practices are the conditions of right diet, right sexuality and right livelihood. The essence of diet is simplicity. First we eliminate drugs, alcohol, tobacco, and television (one of the most addictive and destructive of drugs) from our diet, with occasional exceptions that are appropriate to certain times and uses. Then, so as not to shock the body, there is a gradual movement from a heavy diet of meat, chemicals and dead food to a lacto-vegetarian diet, (with random but infrequent use of dairy products), low in carbohydrates and tending towards raw food over time, without a strict reliance on dietary fads or supplements. But more important than what we eat is how we eat.

The ultimate healing consideration is that if we rest in Organic Innocence then essential health is what arises. Adjustments are made in relationship to the context of health, but are not remedial. Health is the recognition of who we are, not a curative or symptomatic psychology; and good company, right livelihood, right living are the appropriate context for health.

As we eat with attention, we become sensitive to the body's signals as to when we should eat, when we have eaten enough, when we need to vary diet, etc. Different types of people by disposition require a different balance of qualities in their diet, but essentially moderation and appreciation become the mode of everyone's approach.

The aspect of eating in the company of one another is one of the most important aspects of a human and elegant culture. Without making these things the focus, coming together to eat in a benign atmosphere is one of our greatest opportunities for sharing camaraderie, gratitude, generosity, communion, an appreciation of the benediction of the spiritual Master and the simple enjoyment and pleasure in eating good food. The mood of gardeners, cooks, servers and even those who clean up afterwards is as important as the mood we bring to eating. A meal can become a sacred occasion, an actual prayer of gratitude, beginning in the actual growing of the food, through its preparation and in its serving. A lot of complicated and intricate ritual, as traditionally embraced in many sacred cultures is not our way. Lee suggests we replace ritual (though we do employ specific prayers at certain times which Lee has instructed us in) with the ordinary and obvious elegance and sanctity that arises from our bodily submission to the Primacy of Natural Ecstasy.

The mood of eating should be celebration and the eating of wonderful food has always played an important part in the culture of the Hohm Community. As Lee has said, "The only thing to look forward to is dinner."[2]

To begin to consider right sexuality we first need to consider the tendency to promiscuity. Promiscuity is the intuitive move to recreate the Primacy of Natural Ecstacy, from ego's point of view. We are always attempting to find love, but it is only when we rest as Organic Innocence that our movement *is* love. And the best way to observe our search for love is to responsibly engage in a monogamous relationship, recognizing the need to serve and commune with one individual in order to undermine the neurotic movement to "freely" express love to anyone of the opposite sex. The "free" movement that we feel is only the instinctual

[2]Lee Lozowick, *The Cheating Buddha,* (Hohm Press), p. 33

reaction to our refusal to *be* love. So we need a dedicated commitment, one that takes into consideration the possibiltiy of children, and more important that takes into consideration the seriousness of being in the company of the spiritual Master. This takes a conscious agreement to participate with heartfulness, gentleness, generosity and openness.

There are such things as organic celibacy and organic homosexuality, but these are extremely rare. The sexual dispositions that people approach the community with, whether they are monastic celibacy or homosexuality or heterosexuality all arise from the same kinds of contexts as promiscuity—they are strategies of survival and the search.

We are simply not prepared for relationship, and most of us come to spiritual life immature, not yet responsible for our vital and emotional lives. Our movement to relationship is based on insecurity, desperation and clinging need. And, of course, when we approach someone with insecurity, we aggravate the need to be stroked. We would *rather* have ego stroking than the free and spontaneous manifestations of love.

The entire society is playing out a dreadful drama of man/woman relationships and we are part of that acculturation, whether we like it or not. Women have become the men in our society, men no longer know what it is to be a "real man", aberrations of sexual behavior multiply as people seek to experience their lost Innocence (which one can't lose but can bury deeply) and try to uncover it through any means possible. As we become more jaded and our armor thickens, it requires more and more stimulation for us to feel anything at all.

At the very least, women approach with the tendency to mother, control and emasculate men and men to treat women as property and to crush sentiment through ridicule and sarcasm. Lee has said that the primal mood of man is anger, and of woman fear. This is not a very good place from which to begin a relationship! But it is what we come with and we have to begin somewhere.

First we must study the Teaching, then we can begin to embody it. Lee has made the men's and women's cultures the vehicles for our maturation as men and women. We have tested it out—women mature best in the company of other women and men in the company of men. We can't fool one another and we find, as women that we don't *need* a man to be a woman; as men, that we don't *need* a woman to take care of us. This has given the appearance that couples are not supported, but real relationship has always been supported by Lee. It is just that very few relationships have survived the scrutiny of an objective eye—their foundations were usually based on neurosis. It has been demanding work for couples to maintain relationships in Lee's company, but we are now seeing the fruits of his refusal to compromise the vision of the sacredness of relationship between a man and a woman. The couples that exist now have been tempered in His fire and know a profound gratitude for what they may never have known in any other circumstance. When we become Men and Women without the need for consolation, we can bring a fullness and joy to relationship that is as rare in the world as enlightenment.

Lee does offer a consideration of the role of awakened sexual energy, conservation of orgasm, the whole movement of ascending energy in the transformation of the nervous system and other such 'esoteric' subjects, but only to those resting in the context of maturity as students of this way. To awaken and properly use sexual energy, there must be a conscious process of communion, and this is not acquired overnight, nor without surrender, devotion and obedience.

The recommendations concerning right livelihood include a right relationship to work, money, and society. Except for the condition of tithing to the School, they are simply a common sense approach to these areas of our life. Tithing is the reasonable financial relationship we bring to our involvement in spiritual life. Our recommendation is that a minimum of ten percent of one's gross income be tithed to the community, with larger amounts sometimes accepted. Lee has often refused offers of money and goods knowing how soon the 'sincere' donor will turn sour and vindictive. Our financial relationship to the School is directly related to our relationship to practice and life itself. Do we acquire money to acquire security, to use to release tension, to waste, or do we use it in the service of the Teaching? Lee has said that our relationship to money is exactly the relationship we have to energy and modern culture is extremely wasteful of both. Money is a means for obtaining a basic simplicity of survival, after which it should serve the culture that one is part of. We have to choose whether our work and financial resources are to serve the spiritual culture we consider ourselves part of, or whether we still wish to support the abuses of the culture at large, glorifying our ego in the process.

In line with this, we should be discriminating in the kind of work that we do. Some kind of service or the creation of positive goods are sane choices, but if we simply remember to bring integrity and honesty to these areas of our lives, such choices will be obvious. (We highly recommend the books of such critics of contemporary society as Ivan Illich, author of *Medical Nemesis* and *Deschooling Society* and E.F. Schumacher, author of *Small is Beautiful*.)

We work very hard in the Hohm Community. It is an area that demands an attitude of service, surrender and ease and Lee has used it extensively to show us the reluctance we have in giving our energy to life and relationship, and the sheer pleasure there is in having "put in a good day" as part of the natural and easeful activity of an enlightened culture.

One of the most important initial or student tools of Lee's Teaching is in his description of the cycles we move through as we align ourselves to the Great Process of Divine Evolution. Very simply, beginners manifest the cycle of *Infatuation—Indifference—Doubt*, which matures into *Insight—Frustration—Remorse* at the level of basic human maturity, and *Free Moment—Disposition of Unenlightenment—Compassion* at the level of the heart.

Before we are established in the disposition of enlightenment, we repeat these cycles over and over until we pierce the illusion that these ups and downs are exclusive unto themselves and not simply aspects of a process that enables the disposition of enlightenment to manifest in *its* own form rather than the form of the desperation of ego trying to survive or avoid extinction—even as survival is not at all at issue.

High cycles and low are equally enticing in their narrow definition of whatever we are experiencing. We are habitual creatures and creative only in the manifestations of the same patterns. It requires a great leap, great transcendence to rest in a disposition of equanimity. First we need to observe these patterns that prevent the leap.

When we first approach spiritual life we are riding high on the *infatuation* of something new and exciting. We feel good about finally acting on what we have recognized; we have found the beloved Master and have seen through the snares of the world; we feel completely committed and sure, ready to jump in wholeheartedly. But because our enthusiasm isn't based on a solid foundation of understanding, *infatuation* is quickly followed by a period of *indifference* and then *doubt*. This is the common pattern to our relationships, to life in general and what else do we bring to spiritual life than what we are now, not what we hope to be? Enlightenment is already true of us, yes, but our bodies, our thoughts, our emotions, are in constant conflict. We come to spiritual life because we know we are suffering the ache of the illusion of separation from God and that we need help. We need to go through the process of aligning all these aspects of ourselves so that they don't mask and inhibit our Organically Innocent condition. But after the initial blush of *infatuation* we tend to forget that that is why we came.

Indifference is the defense mechanism to the apparently inevitable disillusionment that follows *infatuation*. It is the cushion between *infatuation* and *doubt*, keeping us from crashing quite so hard. If we have involved ourselves with the School, we recognize very quickly that our view of spiritual life, the community, Lee and ourselves has been very idealistic, tinged by what seems like the again, inevitable expectations. These expectations themselves are a function of an uneducated, fickle, and self-absorbed ego-process. We aren't yet able to see with objectivity and rather than recognize our own immaturity, the pattern is to transpose it onto our vision of the community. We see distasteful things going on that, in our vision, aren't supposed to. We observe gossiping, selfishness, irritability in other students and forget that we have, at least, all of those things too. These same qualities are usually buried a little deeper in the new student and simply haven't surfaced yet, partly because we remain on good behavior for at least the first few months. Then the things that we have been hiding start to rear their ugly heads. In *indifference* we can remain above it all for a time by numbing our essential response mechanisms, both life-positive and life negative, but *doubt* inevitably sets in. The community is just immature and we feel superior; the spiritual Master isn't living up to what we think a spiritual Master should be; and maybe conventional life wasn't so bad after all—we do remember feeling happier before we entered spiritual life, at least we could relieve the tension every once in a while, even if the relief took the form of toxic enervation. We need to pierce the cycle of *Infatuation—Indifference—Doubt* and the tool is Paying Attention and Remembering.

In time we don't stay quite so long in each of the phases because we are able to pierce them sooner—the process quickens. But the cycling has not come to an end and we find that we have succumbed to a different pattern, or really, a more mature understanding within the same pattern—*Insight—Frustration—Remorse*. *Infatuation* has become *insight* and for a period of time we are able to ride high on the *insights* we are having about ourselves and our work. And our *insight* into *others* has become profound! We are as capable as the spiritual Master in describing the shortcomings of others. We begin to feel ourselves as the observer of life; we become detached and spiritually sensitive for periods of time. Our vital recoil seems to easefully dissolve in moments of clarity. This phase must be used to turn *insight* to ourselves, keeping in mind with some objectivity that *insight* doesn't directly or immediately lead to permanent change. *Insight* is invaluable, and can move us into real work, if the mind is observed in its desire to hold onto *insights*, keeping them from becoming action. This period, too, collapses in on itself as *infatuation* did, and we are soon *frustrated*. Our *indifference* was a mask, a cover, and just beneath it lies *frustration*. We are so insightful, we see that *insight* isn't by itself changing us and doesn't necessarily push us to act! Each cycle is a trap in itself, if we assume the cycle is an isolated bubble over and against a more undiffused whole, but also has great value for our spiritual work if we are educated in how to use it and remain lucid in our perception. We are *frustrated* that we can't act on our *insight*, that even when we know certain things to be true, we find ourselves almost blindly choosing habitual patterns instead. It is only a matter of time before this turns to *remorse*. When we were in *doubt*, we could leave spiritual life on the basis of the criticism of the other, now that we are feeling *remorse*, it becomes an opening to leave because *we* are not good enough or strong enough. Or *remorse* can simply bog us down in our own self-involvement and self-importance. If we have not pierced *remorse* completely, we will return to *insight* and *frustration*.

Insight, in time, becomes a spontaneous bodily process and manifests as a *free moment*. We see what is true, it is obvious, and all of the intention surrounding *insight* melts into a natural Realization of the Great Process of Divine Evolution. We are literally, bodily enlightened in these moments, but the process is not yet complete and we have simply entered a new cycle of *Free Moment—Disposition of Unenlightenment—Compassion*. We haven't permanently surrendered to our already present enlightenment. The chaotic and disjointed feeling of *frustration* is now merely the mediocrity of unenlightenment, a state of neutrality that demands divinely Influential Help, yet also is the plateau out of which *compassion* can arise. We are no longer completely self-possessed and have grown out of *remorse* in the recognition that we are not different from anyone else. There can now be a true expansion in our beings to embrace others, to know real *compassion* for the suffering of others, even recognizing at the same time that everyone fabricates suffering for himself. There is no longer arrogance in relationship to the suffering of others, as though they were doing something we don't and that makes us superior. We have run the gamut of self-inflicted pain ourselves and in this knowledge, we become able to serve, in humility and even a kind of sorrow. The maturity at this level could be described as the maturity of the heart. The descending energy has purified to the point where the ascending current can be consciously engaged, indicating the process of the opening of the heart. Lee has said "Never look a gift horse in the mouth, and don't ever trust one either."[1] The experience of a *free moment* is often the trap that convinces the student that he is enlightened in the processes of attained freedom, over and against the already present Reality of "Just This." A *free moment* can last minutes, or even weeks and months and nothing is harder than acknowledging that it has faded away into the *disposition of unenlightenment* once again.

When we recognize and become firmly grounded in this cycle, we must transcend it, too, and rest in complete alignment to the disposition of enlightenment as the movement of the Great Process of Divine Evolution.

We can see that even in a lower cycle of understanding we have glimpses of the next cycle or even of complete transcendence. But as long as we are immaturely being carried away in *enthusiasm* or *doubt*, we cannot use one moment of true *compassion* as the evidence that we are now grounded in the heart. Each level must be completely pierced.

[1]Lee Lozowick, *The Yoga of Enlightenment/The Book of Unenlightenment,* (Hohm Press), p. 15.

There are three levels at which one can be involved in the Hohm Community. They are called The Order of Divine Fools, The Order of Ordinary Fools and the Mandali.

The Order of Divine Fools consists of those who write occasionally, who have read our books, perhaps have visited the Ashram, but who's involvement is essentially casual. They might attend a study group once in a while or random celebrations at which a more open policy of invitation is utilized. This Order also includes friends of the community, and may include friends who have other teachers.

"Divine Fools" refers to those who, because of pride, consider themselves exceptions to the inviolable laws of Surrender, Obedience and Devotion. They are willing to sustain the form of some foolishness (being connected with our school) as an attempt to convince themselves of their own maturity, but are unwilling or incapable of a deeper commitment to spiritual life. However, Lee does recognize their support as a first step towards a real understanding of the law.

Ordinary Fools are students who are essentially following the recommended conditions of diet, exercise, study, meditation and tithing. They are called "Ordinary Fools" because of their willingness to be humble and ordinary in their approach, able to recognize the natural and appropriate forms of respect and recognition in approaching a spiritual Master and his school.

Ordinary Fools are willing to recognize that most of the conventions they hold dear are simply effects of conditioning or tendencies developed as a strategy to avoid extinction. They are foolish enough to recognize the inherent meaninglessness of ego's structures and so can embrace the Teaching. They have recognized the need for Help of a special kind and have the maturity to realize what the spiritual Master is, over and against all other alternatives to this Sacred and Innocent

Wisdom. They are the core of the community, whether they live in some other area of this country or some other country, visiting the ashram frequently, or actually live on the ashram. They serve in a variety of capacities, each as important as the other in the workings of a true human culture and recognize the natural protocol appropriate to senior students, spaces, children, Lee and other areas.

The Mandali is the core of senior students who maintain the sacred space and artifacts that surround the Teacher. They communicate the teaching in an organic way through their personal practice and embrace of it, and source the creation of educational materials needed for the various teaching vehicles. These are the students who have submitted themselves to the greatest demand of their Master. They are not better or higher than other students, they have simply found themselves in the intimate, personal circumstance of the Teacher and more is expected of them, "I'm willing to let Divine Fools be assholes, but I will not allow the Mandali to be that despite their frequent attempts to maintain their anal status in the light of the Benediction of My Wisdom and insistent recommendation to do otherwise," Lee recently wrote in a note to all the ashram residents.

Whatever our role is in relationship to the spiritual Master, the Presence of the Enlightened One is a rare and precious blessing. He asks only for our happiness and gradually, over nine years, we are beginning to believe him. We are beginning to see that what he wants for us, what he has been asking of us for years is what we want for ourselves—to be real, to be happy, to be done with our refusal to love and live. He offers us even more than this in our complete surrender to the Will of God—the Consideration of Loving God, the means for the highest kind of human culture and the highest possibility for mankind to be gifted with the presence of Lovers of God.

Lee does not communicate this to us in the way we expect or want. We would like spiritual life to be sane and orderly and calm and *The Living God Blues* explodes such myths. Lee Lozowick is, in his own words, "a dancer, a sculptor, a rogue, and *then* some." God lives in the Hohm Community—are we willing to submit to the Benediction of His outrage?

We invite you to partake of the feast our Master has prepared for you, remembering that as we digest the meal he has offered, that it is a food we're unaccustomed to. Our bodies may feel the glow of pleasure, or a little discomfort at its first taste. Lee's meals are never ordinary—I know, I've been in the kitchen with him and you wouldn't believe what he puts into salad dressings!

Pig

This section consists of essays and talks given by Lee Lozowick over the period between 1975 and 1984. They have been chosen by the editors for their uniquely special flavor and communication. Some of them consist of dialogues between Lee and his students and these express his madcap play with them.

In the midst of the humor and the play, there is a very profound and serious message—"God does not live in the sky." This is Lee's message: we must live our divinity as human beings, with all the juice, vigor, earthiness and sophistication we have as human beings.

Early, 1976

Lee: All one has to do is just enjoy being alive. People approach that as the hardest thing they've ever done, as if effort were required to relax! There is nothing one can *do* about any of it. Just be happy to be alive and *be alive.*

Student: Birth. Death. Birth. Death. The delusion is that it is birth, death, then infinity or heaven. Actually it's just birth, death, birth, death.

Lee: Right! People think that when they die, they are going to melt into this "Great Beyond." Beyond the Beyond, Gate, Paragate...

Student: Rest in the Elysian fields and pop grapes into their mouths, flying around with little transparent wings.

Lee: Seedless grapes.

Student Are there no pits in the Elysian fields?

Lee: That's it! That's heaven. There are no pits in the grapes. All the fruit is pitless. Pitless watermelons. Pitless cantalopes. That's heaven. Did you get that? That's heaven. Oh my God, what an insight! That's heaven, yeah. All the cherries are grown on the trees pitted. Can you imagine that? Big, black Bing cherries growing on the trees, pitted. Oh boy, just livin' on Bing cherries, everyone of them dark and sweet. And you never crack a tooth. (Sigh) Amen.

April 26, 1981

An objective artifact is an object which has become enlivened as an actual expression of God. The process takes place through the devotion and surrender of an individual who empowers that object. The objective artifact is charged in a way so as to touch others very deeply and on many levels, much as the presence of the living Master might.

The first thing that becomes an objective artifact is the body. Then the objectiveness of that artifact becomes subtler and subtler and subtler until the Essence becomes an objective artifact and then you can be said to have achieved eternal life.

Now this becomes tricky because once your body becomes an objective artifact, what do you think that does to sex? You can't go around sticking it in a hole in the wall. When your body becomes an objective artifact, you have to be really careful about what you do with it. If a woman's body is becoming an objective artifact and is not yet "done" and she decides to have a lark with a bunch of guys one night, she would be ripped off from God, and they all might well be thrown into organic turmoil if they weren't ready to be turned towards this God.

What happens in the first stage, when the body becomes an objective artifact, is that you are bonded. If for some reason, you choose to return to conventional consciousness, you might spend the rest of your life in the dark night of the soul. At that point, you are so far surrendered that to come back out of it would be like being wrenched out of a dream. You couldn't live without God, but you couldn't go back into it. It would be maddening. You would either go into profound turmoil or make a new environment for yourself. The turmoil would be a kind of vicarious expression of the pain of disassociation.

So when your body becomes an objective artifact, you become selective; you just don't go making it with every pretty young thing you see, (meaning of course, every pretty young woman, every pretty young boy, every pretty young ice cream cone, every pretty young steak, or every pretty young $100 bill).

When your body is an objective artifact, sex can be an influence that spiritualizes your partner's being. That is very important because if you use that randomly or as a magical form of control, it can be very dangerous. If you have sex with someone who has no idea about spiritual life, you could debilitate them for a lifetime.

Suppose your body had become an objective artifact and you were out in California (Heaven to a great many people) and you were in close proximity to a bunch of naked bodies in a natural redwood hot tub. Someone propositions you. Some therapist says, "Boy, your body is an objective artifact; let's do it." And you say, "What the hell?" When you have sex with somebody and that person doesn't take responsibility for his own spiritual life, he will pull you back to earth next life to work it out with him.

Do you want to come back again, eh?

Do you want to do this all over again, eh?

Do you want to be listening to this trash again, hmm?

Of course not! So watch where you hide the sausage (or let it be hid).

November 5, 1981

What is required to make you a real disciple dredges up so much of you in the beginning stages, you may well feel inadequate for this Work. Some of you are heroic about certain things and you want me to give you spiritual exercises in the areas of your heroism. You know you can do them very well. But that may not be what's needed. You may need to work on other things, but you are not willing to do that. Some of you would like to feel that nobody has gone through this like you are doing. Too bad, too bad. There are numerous people who have gone through exactly this, for eons. You are not the only one, no special case.

You can tell a false school a mile away. Just look at what the school supports. If it supports bioenergetics, massage, loving everyone unconditionally, no discipline, feeling good—you know that people there are not doing real work. Everybody "feels good" in those schools but nobody is doing real work. So don't be fooled. They may appear happy but they will be back to this purgatory Earth a million more times.

You may feel ecstatic sometimes and sometimes very depressed. That is a sure sign that real work is going on. Life is not one-sided. The passion runs the gamut from one end of the spectrum to the other. The Process will be proven out later.

(Lee questions the groups). How many of you feel completely fulfilled at this moment?

(No one raises a hand). Well then, you can be sure that something real is going on.

March, 1979

Student: Has anyone really been able to use you and know what that is?
Lee: People have random flashes of it, but using me doesn't mean coming to Lee and asking advice. You can attack heaven with troops, you can scale the walls, but you need to know what heaven *is* first. There are moments in which people really know how to use me and *do* use me, but the problem is that those moments usually fall into the context of separation instead of the context of Godlife. The context is what is important. It is the base from which we operate. If people operate from a context of separation, of suffering, then they do have moments of Godlife, random moments of incredible rapture, ecstasy, freedom. Yet since the base of their activity is assumed as separation, these moments come quickly and fade quickly. They can't retain what was received in those moments. When the context of our activity is Godlife, those moments of mystical experience still are experienced randomly, but because of the appropriate context, a thread of what is seen in those moments is retained and you continue to use it, even though the ordinary state of affairs is just a natural, easeful and fluid movement through life, free of recoil and the pain of the cramp of separation (and the need to maintain survival in the form of the physical body). That doesn't happen conventionally, since the context is not appropriate, and one is *never* free of the cramp (its overbearing presence is only relieved for a moment). The question is: how do you shift into the appropriate context? Yup. That's the question all right.

February 15, 1981

Do you think all this cosmic stuff I'm considering with you is to make you more than human or something? Do you think you're human yet? Do you think you walk around jealous, petulant, vindictive, angry, and you are *human*? No way, fools. What do you think becoming Divine is? Becoming Divine is being truly human, not floating off in some dayglo rainbow cloud in Heaven.

When we talk about realizing the ultimate Truth, all the things you "should do" are not meant to take away your humanity in some way. All of your "stuff" is not *your* humanness. It's a little bit of Mommy, Daddy, Aunt Mary, Uncle John, your dog, the back of the cereal box. The things you think are your humanity are not *your* humanity. They are simply your conditioning. You are caring and loving randomly and that, only rarely. You still hurt one another, insult one another, batter one another psychically. My entire service to you is an offering of true humanity, not mystical ascension, although that certainly (and incidentally) will be a part of your maturity.

When you are sitting in the same room with someone who is so locked into his idiosyncratic personality that if a bomb went off, he wouldn't be touched by it, and you are sitting there seething, *you* aren't being human either. When you are sitting in the room actively and enthusiastically guarding your territory amongst friends, you may have tremendous alertness, but humanness? Nope.

But I think it's safe to say you all have the potential to be human. You've all got the equipment. You don't need another ear or another eye or a new mind.

Schools that appear to be more human than this one, doing a lot of kissing, touching, hugging, back/ma-rolling, "free" dance, getting together for gestalt sessions, appear more gentle, more loving, yet they are supporting superficiality because they don't deal with the depth of people's true selves. After you've had a good massage, you are never going to think of anything real. You get high, deep and so on but things that need to be dealt with simply aren't. You get mellow and stay asleep.

Schools like ours allow the student to be real at a primal level. It's a passionately raw way. It is the only humanitarian way of being because if we make it through this process in one piece, we will be Real human beings.

June 23, 1983

What I view as pain is the whole process of separation from God. So when I look at people, even when they look relatively happy, it's obvious to me that they are in pain. People do have free moments in which they are very happy and they are not in pain; at least essentially, yet even so, when I look at people, I see their deepest thread of pain. It's very simple. The reason they are in pain, even when they appear happy, is because they are functioning under an illusory assumption. Their whole perspective, (not their intellectual perspective, which is something very lucid and acute and at least rhetorically appropriate), but their bodily perspective is one of the attempt to avoid extinction, which manifests because of *assumed* separation. It's not that you assume you are separate from God because you try to survive. It's because you assume you are separate from God first, you develop this strategy of existing, which is one of avoiding extinction or attempting to maintain survival immortally, eternally.

What I see as pain is the kind of pain that people don't realize and aren't willing to dig for in an objective view of themselves. A lot of people, even when they appear light, look to me like they are in pain, dark and cloudy. Sometimes people can't understand why when they are real happy, I am looking so sad.

When you are suffering, when you are really in pain, you may be willing to investigate, to Enquire and say, "Maybe my life isn't as perfect as I thought it was. Maybe." Or perhaps if you are really sensitive, you will say, "Maybe I need to view my life in a different way." But when you are really feeling great, you are totally unconscious of your motivation in every moment, it saddens me. You assume that you are going to survive forever and you cease to look at yourself at all.

You feel really happy and I am looking sad and you wonder why. I'm seeing your pain. You're obviously in pain, but you aren't willing to look at it in those moments. When you are suffering, you can have a breakthrough. When you are ostensibly happy, it doesn't mean you should throw away the happiness and start suffering. That's just stupid. I'm not suggesting that you take matters into your own hands. You don't understand the truth of things bodily, so don't be dumb and put yourself in a position in which you create unnecessary crisis. That's absurd.

But you know, just going through life without doing anything, you have enough variations in mood and circumstance so that there are times in which you are not walking around feeling ecstatic. There are enough moments of tension, enough moments of crisis or conflict. True? And to varying degrees some people have very little of that and it's natural. Some people have much less than others. For others, their whole life is a problem.

When I look at people, I obviously see two things. I see that people are already Enlightened, but I also see that people are suffering a great deal of pain. They suffer not because they have to, but because they labor under the illusion of separation. That illusion creates the dynamic of the drive to survive eternally in this form. The fact that the form changes is very threatening to most people. You will all see that as you get older. The form changes, you know. The muscles sag a little bit. Breasts sag. Belly flops out. Men get a little gut. It's a terrible thing. Many men go through great existential crises because their gut hangs out a little bit. They are really worried. And the older you get, the more vain you become. The more you begin to look at yourself. You see that your skin is getting a little wrinkled. It causes real crises of reflection because we want to survive *in this form.* We desperately want to survive in this form. We want to survive in this form at our peak, when we are young and solid and juicy. That's how we want to survive.

I see that people are in pain, that even when people appear to be happy, there are hidden agendas. All of you see it too sometimes. You don't need special four-D glasses. You would put on your four dimensional glasses: "Oh my God." And then you take them right off. What a show!

Sometimes you get to see that even when some people walk around looking really happy, you know that if you just said the right word what would happen. How happy could they be? That's what I see when I look at people because I know all the right words. So since I know all the right words, when I look at people that appear to be happy, I see pain because under the surface, they are armed and ready to do battle the minute the right word is said or the minute the right circumstance arises or they see the right look on someone's face or the right tone of voice. And they will cut off their nose to spite their face.

I will always encourage you to look at the way I see pain, because if you begin to see pain the way I see it, you will begin to see that kind of pain is not like having an infected tooth. It's not like physical pain. If you begin to see your pain the way I see it, you will cease to have it. You will cease to have it very quickly. You tacitly recognize what physical pain is. It might not be comfortable, but you understand what it is. And there is nothing you can do about it except go to bed, and wait till it subsides and eventually you get better.

But with the other kind of pain, there is something you *can* do with it. Physical pain is not an illusion, but the kind of pain that underlies your behavior, your activity, *is* an illusion. Not in the sense that it isn't real when you feel it. It is an illusion in the sense that it is based on something that is not true. And if you re-orient what it is based on, then the pain will cease to be true as well. In that way, it's an illusion. If you re-establish the base from which your activity stems, you will cease to be in pain. That's what I would recommend.

May 20, 1984

People often come into my company with an idea, an image of how "the sangha" should be. They expect a certain level of relational integrity, a certain dynamic of "enlightened disposition." Yet these very same people who so blindly assume they are capable of immediately being Enlightened (or already are, just looking for some more good ol' Awakened company), if they only have the Enlightened environment in which to function or plug into, are almost totally unwilling to give any energy or discipline to the creation, implementation, or sustenance of this space they seem to so desperately and passionately desire. These are the very people who are always "entering into a relationship" expecting or willing to give it a month to work, and leaving it critically and disillusioned (once again) when it doesn't. These are the people who make up the divorce statistics (but who usually never get far enough into a relationship for marriage in the official way to even take place) and who assume they are the intelligensia, "the cream of the crop." These are the people who are indicative of the absolute failure of the separative self sense as a viable alternative to the Truth.

People expect to come into my company, to engage my devotees in "relationship" and to get a free ride. But there are no "free rides." To see the Enlightened disposition, to recognize it in others, one must also bring that disposition into the circumstance. One must be this Enlightenment oneself in order to find it here. One must be so convicted of the need to function from the context of Organic Innocence, that no sacrifice (even that of the presumptuous delusions of the self-referencing mind) is too great to create the disposition of Enlightenment in the culture of life. To be willing to give a few months, as an experiment, threatening to "pull out" if it doesn't work, is the height of egotistical and self-deluding (also self-fulfilling, as Ego knows its own safety depends on the continuous failure of such "experiments") braggadoccio. Such arrogance has no place in a spiritual culture. In fact, such arrogance has no place in a human being, but is all too prevalent in the swine of the culture of the illusion of a god in the sky who is distinct from all of His creation. I must suggest that you must pay for the vision you so crassly carry in your mind. You must give to your idea of how things should be, an already present manifestation of patience, compassion, service, dedication, discipline, integrity, creativity, and the freedom of the Primacy of Natural Ecstacy. No less will do. Any less will leave you as frustrated, as angry, as sure of your own deluded "rightness" over and against others' "wrongness" as you are now. And that, as I am sure you realize, is absolutely no way to fly (and even less a way to live).

You cannot come here cramped and crippled in your humanity, bitter from years of unenlightened struggle and complaints, and expect not to have to obviate these nasty characteristics, but to simply be elevated to equanimity and an Enlightened disposition along with all of your delusions and false assumptions. Come to me already happy or be willing to do what is necessary to be happy in the moment. Do not expect everyone else to do it for you, for that is only to court the kind of disappointments that have already made you so distant from life, so cold, so harsh, so defensively and unjustifiably isolated from all that is Real.

If you want to be recognized for your brilliant contribution, be happy and free, live this Enlightened disposition in every moment and cease to eat up your waking hours with the criticism of all those who don't meet up to your expectations. Cease to poison your mind with the pollution of judgementalism, righteousness, and dogmatic differentiation. Be the one who loves. Be the one who serves. Be the one who obeys and you will find Me. Otherwise you will simply continue to wander in the wasteland of your own creation, perhaps even eternally. I wish you more than that. I am here only to offer you more than that. But still you must hear me, see me, Trust Me. Is a life of Organic Innocence, a life moved by Divine Influence, free of the cramp of survival (fear of extinction), a life of already happy and full majesty, worth a little discipline, a little clear observation, a little maturity? Is it? Is it?

Well, if you decide it is, give me a call. If I'm on vacation just leave a message on the tape machine and I'll get back to you when I return. And if having to leave a message on a mere machine offends you...

February 22, 1984

Student: There's a car engine and the oil's never been changed. It's all gunked up. It doesn't run. You bring it into the mechanic and the guy says: "This thing needs a complete overhaul." Or maybe he says, "This thing—forget it. I've got to get you a new block." So it feels like you say things and I try to follow them in my body, you know, the whole thing that you're saying. But it feels like the machine, the engine, is too gunked up with the identification. It feels like...
Lee: It's not the machine that's gunked up. That's the reason there's hope. Wait a minute, there's not supposed to be any hope. *(laughter)* Uh-oh. There's the guru being enigmatic again, contradicting himself once again. Well, it was eight years ago that I said there was no such thing as hope. Eight and a half years ago. *Now* there is hope. *Then* there was no hope. Then? Forget it. But now there is hope.
Student: Possibility?
Lee: No, *(his voice raises to a shout)* hope. *(laughter)*
Student: No hope?
Lee: There is hope but there's no possibility. There is no possibility. there's a possibility of changing hats. But there's no possibility of realizing who you are. I don't like that phrase: "Realizing who you are." Realizing the truth of things.

The fact is that it's not the engine that's gunked up.
Student: What is gunked up?
Lee: No *thing* is gunked up. The process itself creates the illusion of gunked-upness. But in fact, the machine is not gunked up. Sometimes the machine will work less than optimally because the machine is intelligent and can be convinced that it is gunked up. But it is not the machine.

Everything is a matter of the misidentification of the process as a thing, a some-thing, when it is nothing.
Student: It feels as if the process is exactly the same day after day. Is

the process constantly recreating itself?
Lee: Yes. The process constantly recreates itself.
Student: How? What is the Process? Is it the mind identifying...
Lee: How? How? How? *(He speaks to the questioner.)* Are you getting nervous? Why?
Student: Because I'm asking too many questions.
Lee: Why?
Student: I don't know why.
Lee: Why do you *feel* like you're asking too many questions?
Student: It feels out of place.
Lee: Why?
Student: Uhm...*(pauses)*
Lee: *Even if I say it's not out of place, it still feels out of place to you, true?*
Student: *Yeah. A little bit.*
Lee: *That's proof that you don't believe that we're really sitting in a field and that there are no walls and no floor. That is the proof. Do you follow?*

(A few students acknowledge yes.) It's proof that you don't believe me because *I* say that's not out of place and yet you still feel that your perspective/opinion is true over and against what *is* true, both by My proclamation and by the dynamic of our discussion. You're inspiring me. *(He shouts these last two words.)* I'm being inspired! It's exactly what I was looking for. You're playing right into my hands. *(He's still shouting.)*

But you are still getting nervous because it feels like you're asking too many questions. Why? Despite the fact that you've brilliantly helped me prove an argument. Why?
Student: Because I looked around to see if others were interested.
Lee: No, other people aren't interested. Other people are sitting there with their hands up and because I'm not acknowledging their questions and I'm dialoguing with you, they put their hands down and they're waiting until I'm finished with you. But they are sitting there so full of their own questions that they're not interested in what we have to say together, no matter how valuable it might be. That's what's going on.
Student: And I would do the same thing and my question...
Lee: People don't realize what a valuable discourse this is. So fuck 'em. Eat shit and die, suckers! *(The group rollicks in laughter)*

(When the laughter subsides) You do, you understand. You *do* eat shit and die. You eat shit all your lives and then you die at the end of your life. What the hell? Life is hard and then you die. *(laughter)* (Both "Eat shit and die" and "Life is hard and then you die" are inscriptions that Lee has on t-shirts which he wears with delight quite often.)

Student: I thought the motto for this school should be "Eat shit and live." *(uncontrollable laughter attacks the groups.)*
Lee: I was going to cover that tonight. That's true. You eat shit *and* you die. The way of sadhana here is to eat shit and live. Does that make sense?
Student: Yes.
Lee: Good. Now we've come to some conclusive realization.
Student: You've got to be a connoisseur about the shit.
Lee: Well, yeah, shit is not what we give one another when we're annoyed. It's not personality clash. "Man, I'm always eating shit." *(Lee turns to another student who appears to be frowning and looking distracted)* What, did you think I was criticizing you?
Student: Yeah.
Lee: I know you did. So get happy. I was paying attention to you. I noticed you! *(laughter)* The spiritual Master noticed you, took you into His consideration, and made you a part of a lesson that will live forever. And will go into the next book. Aren't you pleased?
Student: *(Without much enthusiasm)* Yeah.
Lee: Is your question important? Is it vital?
Student: It isn't a question.
Lee: Is your comment vital?
Student: *(After a long pause)* I thought it might be able to...
Lee: Shed light on things? Okay, you inspire me too. You're playing right into my hands. This is what I'm looking for, you understand? *(laughter)* I've designed this whole thing. I mean, I planned it all out. That's why I left dinner early so I could work out the fine points.

So, you thought you were going to shed light on what the spiritual Master was saying? *(asking with a cynical tone as the student denies with a shake of her head.)* Oh, what were you going to do? Yes you did, but say no anyway. *(He whispers loud enough for all to hear.)* That's just what I wanted you to say. *(laughter)* Why don't you say what you were going to say?
Student: No.
Lee: No? Please? I want you to.
Student: Well, it looked like Purna was confused with the words you were using to describe ego. I had come across a word to describe ego that had a very strong impact. So I was just going to say what that was.
Lee: What is it?
Student: Uh-oh. Now she's not going to say it.
Student: I'm not going to say it. *(laughter)*
Lee: I thought you were trying to shed light on what the guru was saying but you're only trying to shed light on what the disciple was saying.

So, that's wonderful. Why don't you help him out?
Student: I don't remember now.
Lee: You can remember if we both try. Okay, what is it. You can close your eyes and turn your face to the corner if you want.
Student: *(After a long pause)* That ego was an activity.
Lee: An activity. *(pause)* Does that help? *He asked the original questioner.)*
Student: Yeah.
Lee: Ya see? *(he shouts) (laughter)* Do you see?

The word that shattered the silence. If Meher Baba had only said that before he died...ACTIVITY...and waves of nothingness would have flowed around the earth and nothing would have happened. That's why he didn't speak before he died. Nothing would have happened.
Student: What is the thing that relates to that activity? Is it the mind? It's not the machine. What is the thing that identifies so tenaciously with that activity?
Lee: It's the mind.
Student: The mind. The thinking process?
Lee: The mind. The thinking process is too narrow a definition of the mind. The mind identifies with it and the mind wills the rest of the functions of the organism-body and emotions to keep it really simple—to follow its direction, its identification.

So, the body and the emotions have no mind of their own, and they need a mind. They act like they have a mind of their own. Certainly. *(laughter)* They simply assume that the mind that has made that misidentification, as if it were their mind, it's mind, and that's why the whole thing functions without conflict. Internal conflict galore, but without conflict in relationship to the illusion, the identification as the hat.
Student: Body and the emotions identify with the mind?
Lee: Yes. Some of you are hats with little...have you ever seen those beanies with the things that spin around? We have visitors come like that all the time. Remember the fruitarians that came? They were beanies with things on top. *(laughter)* That's the kind of hats they were.
Student: What, in terms of our childhood education makes that assumption? Can we be raised in a way so as not to make the assumption of identification as the hat?

Lee: One can academically be raised not to make the assumption, although pragmatically that is practically impossible. One can be raised, though, to redefine oneself on the basis of resting in organic Innocence at a certain point in time. One can be primed to wake up, in other words.
Student: Would that describe the process that goes on here?
Lee: That describes the process that we are attempting to acculturate,

that we are always experimenting in relation to.

Student: But if you say it can't be done academically, then it's impossible?

Lee: Didn't *I* just say that? How can one grow up without being conditioned in some way?

Student: You couldn't create an isolated environment?

Lee: No. First of all, the identification takes place so early in life that no form of communication that an adult could make to that early form of life would be intelligible. And then, who would want to live in such a sterile space?

There is a way of putting in a kind of timing mechanism so that it will trigger at some point. That was something else I wrote down to discuss tonight.

You see, I am your nervous systems. Were you observing the sympathetic play that was going on between myself and several devotees while people were offering prasad? I am your nervous system. One of the things it behooves you to consider, behooves...*(laughter)*

Maybe if we were all behooved, the men would grow hairy legs and tails and horns. Where would we find some Sabines? Maybe in Matt's Saloon, or the Owl Bar? Sounds like a good opening line: "Hello, are you a Sabine?"

"What the fuck is a Sabine?"

"Am I a Sabine?"

"No, you shit. I left my Sabine home."

"Don't get wise or I'll shoot it up your ass."

Student: What's a Sabine?

Lee: You know, what the satyrs chase, the nymphs, the ones those hairy hooved dudes chase and rape. Of course, they were created to be chased and raped so you couldn't call it rape, whatever the satyrs do to them.

Haven't you seen all those beautiful...who painted pictures like that? Rubens. Rubens painted women who looked like Sabines. Funky thighs and breasts.

Student: The Mona Lisa?

Lee: No, Rubens didn't paint the Mona Lisa. *(laughter)* Who *did* paint the Mona Lisa? Rembrandt? No, Da Vinci.

Student: Mr. Moose?

Lee: Ah, the truth comes out. *Moose* painted the Mona Lisa. *(laughter)* That's why she had that smile on her face. She said, "I know where he got *that* from." That's why she could only smile with half her mouth. The other half was in pain.

So, it behooves us to sympathize with, to recognize that I am your nervous system. You see I never have any experiences. I *never* have *any*

experiences. I never have any insights. I never go into samadhi. I'm never in bliss. Nothing ever happens. I just go along the same way all the time.
Student: How does that prove that you are our nervous systems?
Lee: How does that prove that I am your nervous systems?
Student: I asked you first. *(laughter) (Saqi pauses, then asks with a thoughtful tone amidst rollicking laughter from the group)* How does that prove it? This is a stalk of rhubarb. *(long pause)* That's how it proves it. *(he's grinning with a devilish glint in his eye.)*
Student: He'll make you eat the sucker.
Lee: You know, this is going to ruin a lot of us. A lot of us have been walking around for years not having spiritual experiences saying. "It's just tendency." And the guru doesn't have any spiritual experiences.
Lee: Well, maybe those of you that don't have any spiritual experiences are perfectly attuned to the spiritual Master.
Student: Is it in the experiential realm, of being your nervous system.? *(The group explodes in laughter as Saqi continues to play with the rhubarb stalk.)*
Lee: Yes. *(the laughter intensifies)*
Student: Is it in the non-experiential realm?
Lee: No. Wait a minute, I'm supposed to contradict myself. Yes. Ooooohh. *(Lee stabs himself with the rhubarb stalk as if committing Hara kiri.)*
Lee: So...*(the phone rings in the next room.)*
Student: You could say you're not home.
Lee: Who is it? Go ask who it is. Then maybe we'll put Lalitha on.
Student: *(In a whisper)* It's Dave, man. He's got the stuff. *(laughter)*
Lee: It's Dave?
Student: He's one of the owners of the aloe company. You can work with him anyway you want.
Lee: Okay, you can talk to him.
Student: He knows all about this stuff.
Lee: He does, eh?
Student: Oh yeah. *(and then he leaves to answer the phone.)*
Lee: Little does Dave know that he just put off Purna's enlightenment for fifteen years. That son of a bitch. Wait 'til Purna finds out.

Anyway, when you realize that I am your nervous system, you realize that if you can sympathize your nervous system with mine...I'm not your nervous system in the sense that I can intentionally manipulate the mechanics or the electricity of your experience. But this nervous system *is* your potential. Whatever you are born to be, given all the factors of your appearance here: your disposition, the stars, the numbers, the creases in your palm, the bumps on your head...

Student: The head between your shoulders...
Lee: The yellow streak up your back...
Student: The toe jam between your toes, the braids in your armpits...
Lee: The sea of warm oatmeal between your ears, that dull lack of glimmer in your eyes, the tunnel of darkness where your eyes should be...you see, given all of the aspects of your appearance here, each of you, as an individuation of God, has a certain optimal possibility, in your few seconds of existence...in your instant *(Lee snaps his fingers)* of existence.

You have a certain possibility. The first conceivable consideration that you might realize that possibility, is that you're here. So you've already got a chance, one up on the eternal round of ordinary existence, a "jump on destiny." Without being here, no chance. Or, in the company of someone else who manifests the same circumstance, the same *(pause)* whatever it is. It's a whatever-it-is. We don't know what it is. It doesn't make a difference anyway.

Given that I am, for each of you, that potential, I cannot, with an effort of will, well actually, I *can* by an effort of will, as you were observing earlier, manipulate even in the solidest of you, I can manipulate, if I put my attention on you and do a little magic, I can manipulate the circuit of energy in your body and the chemistry of things.

However, it would be absurd to think that I had the foresight to be able to recognize what each of your optimal potential was exactly, and to create that in you. I'm not a computer. I'm not the akashic records. Personally, individually...this one who serves you through His *sacrifice,* through His already present sacrifice...it's not like, "Oh, I see a devotee who needs some work. I think I'll sacrifice for him." The sacrifice has already been made. It's not made all the time. It's already been made. It's too late.

Oh shit. I *just* had my first insight. Maybe it's not too late. Maybe I can go back to sleep *(he exclaims in an excited voice.)* Oh, maybe I can find a Teacher and be an important student in the work. Well, maybe I can run a study group.

No, I can't. Forget it. *(dejectedly)* All hope is lost. *(A long pause, then Lee begins to sing a song his twelve year-old son had taught his three year old daughter, a song they sometimes all sang together. The song is accompanied with expressive hand and body gestures.)*

"Little Bunny Fufu, hopping through the forest,
Picking up the field mice and bopping 'em on the head.
And along comes the good fairy and says,
'Little Bunny Fufu, I don't want to see you
Picking up the field mice and bopping 'em on the head.
And if you do it one more time, I'm going to turn you into a goon."

And the next day:
Little Bunny Fufu, hopping through the forest
Picking up the field mice and bopping 'em on the head.
And along comes the good fairy and says:
'Little Bunny Fufu, I don't want to see you,
Picking up the field mice and bopping 'em on the head.
And if you do it *one* more time,
I'm going to turn you into a goon.'
And the next day:
Little Bunny Fufu, hopping through the forest
Picking up the field mice and bopping *(punching with great gusto)* 'em on the head.
And along comes the good fairy and turns Bunny Fufu into a goon.
And the moral of the story is: Hare today, Goon tomorrow."

The way it works is that, if you sympathize yourself as *my* nervous system, the potential of your destiny will be realized through the fact that, and the essential realization and truth of the matter, that I am your nervous system and everything it entails because I am the ultimate dynamic of existence. And not only am I that, physically and literally, but I am also the realization of *your* particular potential, of your unique destiny. If you become what I am, you unlock the door to your personal universality.

The unlocking of the door is *already* the realization of it, given some time lag for the body and all of its components to catch up.

Student: Is that ever an actual, physical transmission?

Lee: Yes.

Student: That becomes, not independent of but actually more than a mere discipline?

Lee: Yes, yes. I like the word independent because it is a physical transmission that separates you from me in a way that you need to be separated from me eventually.

I don't want all of you in my spines. You know what I mean? Tickling my chakras while I sleep! *(A little song and dance ensues, with finger snapping...to the tune of "I got you under my skin")* I got you, up in my spine..doo..doo..doo..doo..

Student: So is that the answer to the question? We kind of got to a climax before...

Lee: We did? *(he asks in a tone indicating something fabulous has totally passed him by)* Oh *shit.* God, damn, I miss everything.

Student: There's the process of ego, mind identifies with it and translates it to body and emotions...what pierces the mind? What pierces that rela-

tionship? Are you saying that what pierces that relationship is the process that you just described now?
Lee: Yes.
Student: That's it?
Lee: Right. Without Me*, kids, back to TV land. Without Me, you're just on TV, being entertainment for children of a different sort who are watching you, whose parents are too bored or too busy to pay attention to them. And they're plopped down in front of the set, hypnotized by your mechanicalness and your predictability. You are just part of the script, a celluoid image.

There are children watching you right now absolutely as fascinated by you as your children would be if you put them in front of the TV and allowed them to watch Mighty Mouse or Krazy Kat.

It's exactly what's happening. You're entertaining children, hypnotizing them. If you have the least bit of compassion in your heart, you have to make a sacrifice for those children. You have to smash the set. You have to break their dependence on the hypnosis you produce in them and you do this by waking up. You will save an entire culture in the process and probably be worshipped as some great Divine Spiritual Ascended Entity-Master when it's just little ol' you!
Student: Is that the transmission that is made in every lineage or in this one?
Lee: In every lineage.
Student: Even in Zen?
Lee: Yeah, sure. *(with a smirk)* It must be. What else could it be? There's nothing else it could be. Well, there is something else it could be.

There is the transmission that allows us to be conscious beings and there is the transmission that turns us into eternal toads.
Student: I must have got that one last time. *(laughter)*
Lee: *Why? Do you have warts? Well, we have a very good healer that... Both transmissions are made here. This is the point of departure in both directions.*
Student: *I don't understand.*
Lee: *This is the point of departure to consciousness and this is the point of departure to being conscious. As a human incarnation, we are sitting on the tangent point.*
Student: *Will we become both or just one?*
Lee: *We'll become one or the other, or remain on the tangent point.*

**Every once in a while, the Master refers to himself in the same tone that Krishna used in his discourse to Arjuna, as the Universal One. Thus the capital M, though usually when the Master says "me" he just means "me".*

Fox

February 21, 1984

Lee: Okay, Mick. *(he speaks to one of the women wearing a plaid Irish country hat).* Alphonse! *(to another student in a beret).* You know who that hat makes you if you weren't in My company? *(to a student in an oversized "hip" hat pulled down over her face in a rakish manner)* Suzie, of course. But in My company...
Student: I would *never* wear this hat when I was Suzie. *You* gave me this hat. *(laughter)*
Lee: That's why, in My company...
(A devotee raises her hands over her head in ecstatic embrace of the universe)
Lee: Isn't that what they do when the ball goes over the goal posts. So what does that mean in here, eh?
Student: Stick 'em up. *(The room rollicks in laughter)*
Lee: So you still have a question?
Student: No.
Lee: Discretion is the better part of valour. Good for you. Description is the better part of valour. *(He yells at the group)* Inspire me! Inspire me!
Student: I've been thinking a lot about...
Lee: You have. Too bad. What has that brought up? *(laughter)*
Student: I was wondering what would it mean not to have a life of one's own.
Lee: What would it mean to not have a life of one's own? To be dead. *(laughter)*
Student: Really?
Lee: Well, what does dead mean? Dead means alive in one sense. And dead means nonexistent in another sense. And dead means having changed form within exactly the same context in a third sense. Which do you mean?
Another student: You're the one who said dead.
Lee: I am? *(with an incredulous tone)* Which do I mean? *(laughter) (He*

asks the original questioner) Do you see the difference.
Student: Yes.
Lee: Okay, pick the right one and you have your answer.
Another student: (moaning and groaning) Oh no.
Lee: To not have a life of one's own is to cease to identify with the machine as the hat. To cease to identify *as* the hat is to not have a life of one's own.

A student has just arrived and offered as prasad a hand-out form from a group he was visiting earlier in the evening. The Master begins to read it silently and then...
Lee: Oh yeah, this is sick. I thought it might be something like this. Chief went tonight to investigate some "Tantric something or other" and this is sick. I am sure they are very nice people but what dark and awful things were they talking about?
Chief: *(laughter)*
Lee: What propaganda were they filling people's heads with?
Chief: The lady just sort of gave a basic kind of eastern philosophical rap. She was a student of the Vedas. She talked about what Tantra means and what yoga means and what dharma means and the different kinds of dharmas that animals have. And how human beings have Bhagavat dharma which makes them different from animals...
Lee: Dharmas that animals have? That fool. *(he exclaims with disgust).* Who would ever think that an animal had a dharma? We would never think anything like that. Next she'll be suggesting toads can be devotees or something equally absurd. *(wild laughter)*
Chief: She defined dharma as qualities. So she was talking about eating, sleeping, procreating and fear as being what animals have. And human beings have the ability to realize it's all God. So she was just talking about how everything's God.
Lee: Trash.
Chief: And we did a little meditation and we sang a couple of those songs. And they're really into that mantra.
Lee: *(Singing from the sheet in his best off-key voice)*

"I love this tiny green island, Surrounded by the sea. *(Then in a dead pan voice)* Repeat. *(laughter)*
"Touched by the sea. Decorated by the sea. *(Dead pan again)* Repeat.
"Am I a secluded figure in the vast. A little, a meager. No, no, no, no. I'm not alone. *(crescendo) (laughter) (Deadpan again)* Repeat."
(He looks up from the paper and shouts to the group)
Can you guys believe this?

Chief: She smuggled the Mexican scarf, from over the border, up her nose. *(referring to the group leader's attire)*
Another student: An ancient yogic practice?
Lee: Using her black scarf for Nadi, eh?
Student: How do you get it around, up through your nose and out the other side?
Lee: You can bring it in your nose, up one nostril, and out your mouth. Then they have one practice where you swallow yards and yards of muslin cloth and it goes into and through your whole intestinal system. Who wants to taste all that mucus after it soaks up all the crud?
Student: It comes out the other end.
Lee: *(Increduously)* Out your asshole? *(The room explodes in laughter)* Well of course, that's where the thrill comes from. *(General mayhem in the room)* All r—i—i—i—ght—t—t—t—! *(People are still screaming in laughter)* Sounds good! It sounds good. That's what they mean by multiple orgasm. *(uproarious laughter)* So yoga *is* good for something after all. I'm glad we've had this discussion tonight. That's why I created yoga. You do know that I created yoga, don't you. The whole 5,000 years was for this night. *(His voice raises to a shout. Everyone in the room is doubled over in laughter)* Swami this, and Swami that, and Baba this and Hobo this and Booboo this and Bimbo that. Inspire me! *(He shouts again)* Inspire me!

(One student raises his hand and the Master acknowledges him.)
Student: This is not inspiring.
Lee: You never can tell.
Student: Considering what we've been talking about, does...when that comes to fruition?...
Lee: You mean the nervous system thing?
Student: Right. When that comes to fruition...
Lee: More fruits.
(A slap is heard in the back of the room.)
Lee: Was that a mosquito? Oh God. You've just destroyed my whole discourse on the Mosquito and the Windshield. *(laughter)* You've just erased a part of history. Oh God.
Student: Do we know what we're talking about?
Lee: Yes.
Student: Does any other form of life besides an Awakened human being know that?
Lee: No other form of life on earth. *(One student is hysterically laughing through this questioning.)* No other form of life on earth that we recognize to be a part of the animal kingdom. There are other forms

recognize to be a part of the animal kingdom. There are other forms of life on earth, subtle forms of life. There are subtle forms of life that have the ability to self reflect. But they're just as asleep as we are. Although they have a different or a broader kind of wisdom than we do. Their identification is simply with a different kind of hat. We identify with one kind of hat. They identify with a different kind of hat. Have you ever seen those hats that are made out of clear plastic. They are perfectly clear. That's the kind of hats that they identify as.

Student: I can feel what I'm feeling tonight and I know that I'm going to Phoenix tomorrow to see health food stores all day and it seems so inconsistent.

Another student: Maybe you're *not* going. *(laughter)*

Another student: You're going to be stuck in this field tomorrow...

(A student who has arrived late): What's that from? It sounds familiar...being in a field...

Lee: Being in a field?

The late arrival: Yeah, we're all standing in a field and nobody's got clothes on and some of us...

Lee: Are you kinky or what? *(laughter)* We're standing in a field and no one's got clothes on but one person...*What* are you talking about?

The late arrival: Standing in a field....

Lee: But I never said anything tonight about no clothes on. Maybe I should have, eh, if it would have kept your heads on straight?

Student: So what's the field?

Lee: That's what you play when you're *really* suffering.

Student: What?

Lee: The field. *(laughter)* There, you see, you inspired me. Of course, what you'll be doing when you're in the business world is being busy! Probably more busy than you are now. But the business will not produce the kind of ecstatic tension that it produces in you now. And maybe she'll keep you in bed all day tomorrow. *(He points to the questioner's mate.)* Better than going to any ol' Phoenix, *(he says in a sassy voice.)* Then the phoenix will arise in a different context. *(laughter)* She'll make it a sizzler and out of the ashes will arise—the PHOENIX! *(in a dramatic tone.)* So, did we come to a conclusion about your question?

Student: Yes.

Lee: To take another tack. Without any diplomacy...Can we take another tack without any diplomacy?

In work such as this, we tend to forget the real message of the work and tend to assume we're leading spiritual life by *designing* our practice; we've left the world, we're living on an Ashram, we want to be spiritual, but even so, the realization of the truth of things is a very threatening and dangerous consideration so we get lost in disciplines or form.

This is not a dangerous consideration in the conventional sense, but dangerous in the sense of ruin, you see. Dangerous to ego.

We find ourselves in an interesting dilemma. We're here in this School, and we're dedicated to being here. We're here with intention. And we're actually here, many of us, beyond the process of thought and doubt and argument and intellectualization. We're *really* here. Yet we still have the same motivation that we've always had. We still have the motivation to define ourselves as separate beings, as distinct from God, along with the motivation to survive *as* that separate being, over and against God, and play out a kind of search for Divine success, defining Divine success either as worldly success or as spiritual success.

We're still faced with the same dilemma. We still embody the same cramp. And moving into, with intention, this kind of life, we redefine the cramp from the kind of worldly success we once sought, to the form of "spirituality." We have redefined that particular dynamic from worldly success: just the right family, just the right job, and money and security and travel and so on, to the spiritual success: higher and higher experience, functioning from the disposition of Enlightenment, assumption into the highest level of consciousness, realization of Enlightenment, wisdom, realization of nonduality—whatever it is we call it, you see. We've redefined it but we're still *doing* the same thing.

We find ourselves looking for, in spiritual terms, relationship. We're still looking for relationship. Before we were spiritual creatures, we were looking for relationship. Whether we were looking for relationship through sex, money, power, personality...whatever we were doing, we were looking for relationship, ultimately. We're still looking for relationship, except in spiritual terms and there is no such *thing* as relationship. There is Just This.

There is no such thing as relationship, in truth. There's no such thing as sex. There's no such thing as hunger. There's no such thing as any of the forms we chase.

You cannot find ultimate rest through a child, a wife, a husband, a relationship, sex, food, money, power, humility, realization, because there is *attainment* of all of the stages of the Divine Path of Growing Old and maturity in those stages even while there is no such *thing.*

There *is* no such *thing* as sex. *(pause)* That's going a little too far. *(laughter)* There *is* no such *thing* as relationship. There is only God.

When you realize that there is no such thing as relationship, when you realize Just This, when Assertion is what is true of you in every moment, you will find yourself in circumstances in which children, mate, sex, food, money, simply happen to be a part of your circumstance. And those things will, in a conventional or reflective, relative sense, be dynamic and alive and full of the truth of ecstasy and power.

But until you realize Assertion in every moment, you are merely hoping that those things will do what only your realization of God can do. And they never will.

So, once again it behooves you, it befoots you, it betails you (if you want to be a mermaid) to Remember the realization of God in every moment, because that is what *creates* the comfort of circumstance. Instead of looking for the perfect circumstance and thinking that by creating the perfect circumstance that will allow you the ease with which to concentrate on Enlightenment. Or that will itself *be* Enlightenment. The creation of the perfect circumstance is not itself Enlightenment. Enlightenment is itself the essence of the perfect circumstance. The two are not interchangeable.

To mature into or to attain the perfect relationship, has nothing to do with the realization of God. The realization of God *is,* essentially, perfect relationship. Follow? Good.

(He screams to the room) Over the cliffs, lemmings. Into the s—e—e—e—e—a—a—a—a—a—. *(laughter)* Bring your surf boards.

February 21, 1984

Toads don't have the sophistication of suffering that we have. Nor do they have potential for it. When toads sympathize their nervous systems to My nervous system, which in fact does happen in rare cases, there is the potential for toad spiritual Masters and toad devotees. Yup, there are.

You may never have seen one. But I've seen a few. I've spent many, many summers in the woods and I've met some wonderful toad and snake spiritual Masters.

Student: Are they the ones that make that funny noise when you step on them?

Lee: Yeah. That's how I make the transmission of nervous system sympathy through sound current.* What I'm doing is Enlightening toads through the current of sound. That's the current that toads respond to. They don't respond to subtle communications, not to the emotional current or such. Toads don't respond to glance, as you all do.

I can make the transmission to you through glance. You know what the eyes are. You can recognize when a transmission is being made through the eyes. But a toad can't. A toad needs to be sympathized through something grosser than the subtle transmission or an ethereal transmission. A toad needs to be sympathized through sound.

You've discovered what I'm doing when I fart. I'm Enlightening toads. Every time I fart...toads and frogs. So the secret is out.

When a toad reaches that sympathy with My nervous system, he becomes available to transmigration. He can incarnate into a higher form of life.

What do you think—I'm here just for you? That's presumptuous. I

*The Master is referring to the fact that every time he passes wind, (flatulates), which is fairly frequently and fairly noticeably, He remarks, "Yup, got another toad" as if the toad (thrown into toad samadhi and moved on in the evolutionary scale) was making the sound as a result of being stepped on.

realize that you think a lot of yourselves, but really! I'm not only here for all forms of life that you have come to recognize on the planet since you have been alive, but for forms you can't yet imagine.

Student: Years ago, you said that if we are told to do something in the Community, we have to somehow find a way to make it feel like we have told ourselves to do that. So, somehow it feels as if what I have to do is see things as you see them.

Lee: To see things as I see them *is* to see things as you see them. Not to see things as you *think* you see them. The only way in which we do not realize the truth is because we're not conscious of the realization of the truth, not because we don't have it, or know it, or see it, or realize it or understand it.
Student: So, it's not a question of me going over there *(as he points to the Master)* it's a question of this *(as he points to self)* vibrating in the same way that that vibrates?
Lee: There. *(As he points to the student)*
Student: But over here?
Lee: Right.
Student: Can that be done by piercing that whole spacial perspective?
Lee: Your already present Realization *is* the piercing of what seems to obstruct it. Simultaneous attention and Remembrance. *(The Master snaps his fingers) That's* the process. It requires no temporal lag between some understanding and its eventual manifestation. You must tacitly realize that there is obstruction and not focus on the obstruction. Understand its illusory yet almost tangible essence. But what you do now is work on the obstruction when you simply should be being conscious. Just This is all that is required.

November 18, 1981

This is an orientation. You are being oriented to the only sane alternative to the crippling, mechanical and eternally recurring drama that is historically known as "conventional life" and currently known as the "New Age." If you examine your personal past with any degree of objectivity you will recognize—albeit with much resistance, emotional turmoil and disbelief—that you have never been given or educated to a way of life that can offer, even ultimately, fullness of heart, truth of relationship, and happiness in the midst of depressing and Godless circumstances. You have been given, on the other hand, religion, public (or worse, parochial) education, allopathic medicine and drug dependence, social and governmental madness and the "American Dream" (which is the implication that money, sex and a grander facade of material success will give happiness and even Heaven). Obviously you have all tried, even mastered them all, extensively. Let me suggest: they do fail. You are being oriented here to the only real alternative. But is it a viable one, given our state of affairs? Are any of you a Vivekananda, a Milarepa, a Hui Neng, a Sariputra, a Peter, a John of the Cross, or a Mary? Can Real Spiritual Life be True of You? Can this Divine Influence purify you, or more realistically, will you let it? Of course it can, in essence!

My experience has been that it is possible but that the strength, courage and persistence required could be called superhuman. My senior students are in the midst, sometimes Rapturous, sometimes agonizing, of this superhuman (dare I say Divine?) effort. You must decide whether they are deeply enough and profoundly enough full of God, and representatives of True Love, Mercy and Compassion, to be the deciding factor in your choice to pursue this Way and accept my Gift or to leave it immediately. But do not toy with it. Do not play superficial games with it, as if you were deciding on which bathing suit to buy. Live this life of God or run like hell for your conventional and safe existence.

My Fire awaits and it is up to you as to whether it will burn or melt you in Transfigured Ecstasy. Your move.

November 14, 1981

I've stopped coming on all serious-like, as I did the first year we established Hohm. People were getting blown away by the profundity of My verbiage. Now, the more serious you get, the more I act stupid for you. So, given this state of affairs, it's important that you understand that nothing interferes with the Communication I make to you, with Divine Influence. Lee is *not* Divine Influence. "I" can do the dumbest thing I can think of and the Help I offer avails, no matter how goofy the body is. Know that the Communication is being made no matter what the form is. You may sit here every day of the week and you may ask yourself, "What is he *doing* up there?"

Please recognize that I don't, won't, in fact, cannot make it easy for you. Whenever I talk about something, I can be quite convincing; I have the gift of gab, but so what? I study and amass information and play it back to you in my inimitable way. When "I" have an audience, "I" come alive. But I think that it's essential that you learn to recognize true Communication and just innocent fun. It unlocks every sacred door for you, true Communication. And, not only that, it unlocks the possibility of engaging in Real relationship before you die.

I don't want a large following because of my eloquence. If I'm ever surrounded by many people, I want it to be because of the Communication. So I purposely don't make high claims. I like to sneak in here. I don't tell you how profound the possibility of being here is. I won't dwell on how sacred this space is. To me, that is Real and it must speak for itself. If I talk about that, you may be moved by the eloquence of its paradisical implications, but I am not interested in that kind of participation. If you can *feel* the Communication through all the play, then you may stick around.

I suggest that you consider the Communication that is made. Come to a conclusion and hold on to that *felt* conclusion no matter what. You have to recognize the Influence that is available to you. If I become a drunkard, a libertine, a liar, a thief, *nothing* affects that Communication. Once you make a conclusion that your body knows is True, make a vow and hold onto it no matter what.

I do a lot of stupid things. I say a lot of crazy things. I scare many people away. I drag you through mires and I drag you through heavens. Academically, you could realize the fruit of what I bring to you at any time. But hold on. If you hold on for twenty years and realize nothing, hold on some more.

The main thing that's important is that you recognize the Communication that is made. Everything that I say doesn't always have meaning, but recognize the Communication and hold on.

June 13, 1984

"Do as I say and not as I do" is the primary consideration, and principle or basic edict for all new students here. You cannot even begin to understand what I do for several years, at least, so you must deeply consider what I say in an unobstructed, concise, and objective fashion. You must "do What I say" directly, not after impressing it with the artifices and imposing interpretations of your usually subjective and cloudy mentality.

Philosophy as an analytical tool to realize why I "do" what I do will only prove sterile and frustrating. The attempt to accept what I "do" through an act of faith will also prove hopelessly draining and confusing. Knowledge would only serve if you could know but you cannot for quite a while so don't waste time. Act. Do as I say until you are blessed with the benediction of surrender to the Will of God. Do as I say until what I say needn't be communicated through the channel of speech or Teaching.

When your heart reads what I say with My Heart, what I do will be irrelevant, humorous, a Well of Delight.

Do as I say until what I say is received in the silence of Love. Then we may become friends.

June 15, 1984

People have been telling me how to do my job for nine years now, and if I did it the way they all suggest, I would be worthy of the criticism they level at me.

My Work will never conform to the logic of the conventional mind. It (this conventional mind) seeks to have me function as it always has, therefore assuring me of failure to communicate Enlightenment, and it of continuous survival.

My "motives" will always be suspect to all but the heart, always. To the linear mind, to the terrified vital, to the weak and deluded emotions, I will always seem to be wrong, off-base somehow, sinful, egotistical, self-serving. But to the heart I will be seen as I am, the Beloved of the poetry of old, the God of Man, Beast, Spirit, Deva and god.

Frankly My dears, I don't give a damn whether you think my motives are suspect. I rest as the Primacy of Natural Ecstasy, pervasive and inclusive as Organic Innocence.

See Me and Live. Refuse Me and suffer the eternal rounds of the illusions of birth, death, and the possibility of extinction or survival.

I await your Company impatiently. I am the thorn in the side of Ego...I am the Friend of the Heart. Visit Me when you are willing to be happy without reason, free without cause, in Love without definition, and I will grace you with My Gift.

So Be It.

April 6, 1977

I can't "create" your Enlightenment willfully. What you'll eventually realize is that you can't just sit on your ass and wait for things to happen either. If you do, nothing's ever going to be realized, except that nothing happened after all that time.

You have to go out onto the railroad tracks if you want to get hit by a train. You have to go right out on the tracks. If you sit in your living room, nothing's ever going to happen. You have to go out to the tracks and take a schedule with you. Bring a schedule and a sandwich so you don't get bored or pick a track that's not used anymore. The schedule is discrimination.

Obviously you have to choose carefully where you're going to be because if you pick a straightaway, the conductor may see you and he'll stop the train before it reaches you. So you have to hide down by the side of the tracks and when you feel the train coming, you have to run up and jump out onto the tracks. Fitwhewwww— — — — — — — — That's it, if it's a fast train. If it's a slow train, you have to be *really* sneaky. You have to be prepared to jump right in front of the engine.

Most people are standing on the track and before the train even comes, they jump off. They get scared. They decide beforehand that it sounds heroic to martyr themselves that way, that that's a good way to go. It's fast. But then they get scared and when they see the train, they say, "Uh-oh" and they jump off and the train goes on by. And they say to themselves, "Whew! I'm glad I didn't do that. I'm much better off this way. I made the right choice." Zap, Rebirth. (laughter)

Panther

April 18, 1984

An interesting thing happens when people come to the Ashram to live. People hope that I will be wild, that I will make all kinds of work exercises that will tax their power of warriorship. It is my belief that there is only one great tester—TIME. I don't have to test anybody for anything. For some people, *two weeks,* and they are so bored and/or disappointed that they are gone!

Time is the great tester. I don't test students to verify their level of maturity, to see whether they are strong enough to take the next step. I don't have to. Time does it. People become bored, their expectations haven't been met and I don't have to do a thing.

I provide an Influence, a certain kind of help. I provide that help irrespective of my own form. I have the ability to use a variety of forms with some degree of sophistication, yet none of those have anything to do with what I'm doing here on earth. I provide a certain kind of help. That help is present in spite of Lee. This guy *(the Master indicates his body)* and all of his personality traits and born disposition, his stars, his numbers, the creases on his palm, the bumps on his head, have nothing whatsoever to do with the help I offer.

You need to know that I *offer* a certain help. I do not have to give it. Unless of course, you make me give it. Someone can demand this help in a certain way and I must give it. Otherwise, if it is not demanded, I can give it or not, by choice. If you put yourself in a position that you must have this kind of help to live, I must give it to you. In every circumstance, without exception, I must give it. That's what I'm doing here.

November 8, 1981

Since the demand I make of you is a Divine Demand, you are to become lovers. Some of you have been close enough to smell it. Some of you have tasted it. You have a very definite feeling for what I am talking about. Since it is not a humanitarian demand, some of the people in the group will appear irrational or erratic. All of the unspoken demands of community protocol will come to the surface, too, but that's not what I'm talking about.

Some of the greatest Lovers of God looked like they were in more pain than anyone on the face of the earth. Yet if you tried to ease that pain they would say, "Get away from me. I've spent a lifetime to feel this pain for the Beloved."

Here you are being given a Divine Demand. You must be prepared to walk amongst Lovers of God even if you don't understand them or their behavior at all. You have to be prepared to look at the whole picture and *feel* the truth of this consideration.

The more whimsical I am, the more power, the more Benediction you have showered down upon you. It is a transforming Process. When you think that I am too far out, you let me be only a little whimsical. Your recoil is the bind. I have given myself to the human level of things to work from the "inside out." I have seceded from the Heaven of detachment and creation. I have denied Magic to be Helpless, a reflection of your impotence, your self-absorption, your self-possession or a reflection of your Majesty, your Enlightenment. So it is, this wild and insane Process.

Generally, you have only recognized a humanitarian demand. You want to do things to help me in a stodgy, old, conventional way (like your moms wanted to help your pops). But you haven't found out what really helps me. What really helps me is subject to Whim, which is totally irrational.

You have to make your ecstacy sympathetic to Divine Whim. When you allow me the freedom to be as whimsical as God would be, the power showered on you will be absolutely and irrevocably transforming, bright and full of the light and heat of a million suns.

Why do you think our celebrations are such transforming moments? You get really big hearted and let me be a little free. But do you think you could sustain that for years on end? To varying degrees, you all cramp God's style.

There are demands of protocol, and there is the Divine Demand. The principle demand is the Divine Demand. If you went mad tomorrow, everyone would have to make room for you. This is *Real* shit we're involved in! This is no Positive-Mental-Attitude affair.

May 11, 1979

Moses brought his people to the Promised Land. Moses was a perfect bodhisattva. He refused to enter Nirvana until every sentient being had achieved Enlightenment. Moses brought his people to the Promised Land, right up to the gate and sent them in before himself.

I can bring you right up to the gate, but the last moment is your game. You have got to jump through. I can give you the necessary push (shock); in fact, I can give you such a shock, you'll be out in space for eons, but no matter what the circumstance, you still have to bridge the gap. I can kick your ass so hard, you can bridge eight gaps, but you're the one with the toggle switches. I can push you out of the plane, but you've got the parachute and you've got the toggle ropes. You can see the target. You can let go of the toggles and the parachute will catch a wind current, maybe sailing five miles off target and land in the East River or in the middle of Bayonne if you want to, but you're still the one with the controls. You're the one who's got to get that parachute into that little circle. All I can do is kick you out of the plane. I can't land you. I'm even so Goddamn gracious, just to show you how much I care for you, I can be on the ground with the radio, telling you which toggle switch to pull, in case you're an amateur.

That's what Moses did. He led his people right up to the Promised Land and said, "I'm not going in." It's a parable of spiritual life. That's what the Master does.Takes you through the Red Sea, stops all pursuers, eliminates your tendencies, obviates them through sacrifice and devotion and takes you right up to the Promised Land.

You don't go any place, though. You move right in place. Years pass and your hair is getting a little grey and you say, "My, I was twenty-one when I came to this here community. How time flies! Now I'm thirty-four. Goddamn, isn't that something?" You're marching in place outwardly, and inwardly you are becoming quite transformed.

The Promised Land is like that, often elusive. Moses' people kept saying, "Come on, man, our goddamn feet are covered with blisters and we're starving and there is no food anywhere and you're telling us about this land of milk and honey. What's going on, man?" Moses simply said, "I know it's there. God is telling me." So he gets to a mountain and says, "I've got to go up this mountain, guys." And they say, "Come on, will you Mo? Jesus Christ!" Oops, they didn't say that. Jesus wasn't around yet. "Abraham! Give us a break, Mo. God-All-Mighty!"

So Moses went on up the mountain. And the people forgot about him. They made a golden calf. They wouldn't wait for the Promised Land. He came down with the Teaching and he threw down the golden calf amidst all their partying and merriment and convinced them to go on a little further. And finally they got to the top of a hill and *there* was the land of milk and honey. Everyone was shouting, "Goddamn, you were right, you son of a Jewish whore." Off they went, running down the hill. They were hot and thirsty after the desert. Here was rich country, grass and butterflies. The Promised Land.

And you? The golden calf is your beliefs about Enlightenment and the Promised Land is Sacrifice, the Law, the Truth.

May 10, 1979

You have to trust me enough to be willing to put your reputation in My hands. What the hell is your reputation anyway? Where do you aspire to end up one day? Sitting on an ashram, blissed out of your mind, or on Wall Street, making a million dollars a year? You have to be willing to put your reputation in My hands. Not in Lee's hands, in My hands.

What is your reputation? Can you taste it, smell it, feel it? What *is* it? Pierce that feeling that it is *something* and then you can begin to become responsible for Godlife. I have become responsible for you, that is My job. Until you fulfill Godlife through surrender, I'm responsible for you. That's the nature of things. It is an *absolute* Divine responsibility. I have no choice about it. I have been given to this time and place for this purpose.

When you fulfill Godlife and surrender, then my personal responsibility is obviated. You have, then, taken on a portion of My responsibility for everyone else. Essentially you are a co-God of a bizarre sort.

Right now, you're just struggling to have a little peace of mind. You don't want to be responsible for the rest of the nuts in the community. You look at your household and all you see are a bunch of slobs and procrastinators. You don't want to be responsible for all of them. But that's the Law. And the Law is the *only* thing that is *inherently* pleasurable. The Law is its own reward. It is "Self-centered" so to speak. Everything else dies. *Everything* else is sustained, even the pleasurable moments in life, by tension. The life of seeking is grounded in tension. You may think you are happy, but there is nothing but tension underneath it. The only thing that is *inherently* pleasurable is the Law. Believe it or not, it is true. And I know you don't believe it. Why should you?

It's absurd. To think about it linearly, to think about it logically, you must come to the conclusion that it's absurd. It's not even paradoxical; it's stupid, asinine, even diabolical, it's so absurd. Yet it is the Law. It is the only thing that is from the beginning, tension free, without stress, without motivation, without the need to be sustained. It is simply inherently pleasurable and the only Truth. It is Reality.

Because we don't surrender to it completely, we worry about our reputation and God knows what else. We worry about peeing in our pants, dripping spaghetti sauce on our shirt and having our hair ruffled by an open window in a speeding car. You have to be willing to make Me responsible for your reputation. You've got to be willing to put your reputation entirely in My hands. And if I want to rip it to shreds, well, God bless your reputation. Kiss it goodbye and say hello to Heaven!

Ostrich

Late 1976

There are no degrees of Realization. There is God (the Embodiment of Divine reality as the Great Process of Divine Evolution) and there is suffering (the lack of Divine Sympathy due to the illusion of being a separate or isolated entity). The spiritual Master exists as the absolute condition of both. He is the ultimate Reality *and* the ultimate illusion. Those who refuse to see, those who insist on keeping the search for what is already presently true, endure the pain, the suffering. Those who are only interested in God, no matter what this means, get That. There are no degrees, no almosts. There is no being close; just one or the other. You are suffering or you are not.

Which of the two you choose is up to you. The spiritual Master has nothing to do with it, for he only exists as your possibility and your Help, but not as your confidence in choosing, nor as the impetus to follow the choice. Blame Him if you want, and live until you die. Become Him, and "die daily" before you die. Just This.

January 25, 1981

Praying to a dead teacher is about as reasonable as praying to your goldfish. You could sit in front of the tank and float your prasad on top of the water and meditate on the bubbles from the air filter. You could paste a yantra on the back glass and really do it up in style. Or you could have a horny toad spiritual Master and bring him meal-worms or crickets instead of flowers or fruit. Damn, it would be a hell of a lot cheaper, too. Then you could surreptitiously spend your tithe on hamburgers and milkshakes. If you are going to have a dead spiritual Master, you might as well put up a picture of Casper. Actually, I must confess that my own favorite is Ignatz.

June 28, 1983

We are a food source for one another. Of course we relate to one another differently than we do to our beans, you know. I mean after a good meal, you are supposed to belch and that praises the cook. The dynamic is a bit different towards each other, though. We are a food source for which there is no substitution and which is essential for survival. You see, the more mature you become, the more literally necessary that food source is. The more mature in this Work you become, the more absolutely necessary that form of nurturing is. Literally necessary to life and passion and light.

You can fight it as long as you want. You can beat your head against a cement wall till it's nothing but a bloody stump, but that's not going to change the truth. You cannot stay isolated in your own little bubble forever no matter how hard you try to, how "cool" it might seem, or how attractive that bubble is to ego.

Some people, the longer they are in the Community, the more they suffer. "Why won't these people leave me alone?" "These people...it's these people's fault..." Rest assured, it's *not* these people's fault. You can be the healthiest, smartest, wealthiest, most creative person anybody has ever met. I don't care who you are. It's not these people's fault. That's a fact. That's a fact, son.

Suffering is foolish. I recommend you simply be happy and leave the pain to the unconscious.

November 18, 1979

Often there's a tendency to be distracted in some of the "spiritual" activity that goes on around here: the exquisite mudras, the traditional, symbolic mudras and the wildly bizarre ones, as well as everybody's little dramas, the stuff gossip is made of. We've always got something to occupy us. One day it's our mother, the next day it's our child or our housemate, then it's our lover or it's that we have no lover, the next day it's indigestion. Hourly, daily, monthly.

If we stop to pay attention to our lives, we have little short term things: we have a bad meal, we eat too much sugar, there's a lot of pollution in the air, the traffic is heavy today.

We also have weekly problems: housecleaning, the laundry or maybe there's a good movie playing but I don't have any extra cash and payday's not until next Wednesday or Thursday or Friday or Monday.

Then we have monthly dramas. Some that we're aware of, some that we're not aware of: bio-rhythmic cycles and such. We're always watching our charts and our numbers and our palms and our cards and all these things cause a state of disturbance.

Then we have our yearly problems: "spiritual life isn't getting better the way I thought it would" or something like that. God realization, or whatever the hell that's supposed to mean, isn't true of us yet. Awakening or Enlightenment or Satori, already Perfectly present, non-dualistic blah-blah-blah-blah. And we're so busy confronting all of these temporary problems that we never slow down enough to see what's really going on.

We have yearly problems too, called birthdays. That means we get one year older. When you're twenty-six you don't care if you get one year older. When you're thirty-five, unless you've totally ignored generations of programming stored in the very chemistry of your cells, you start to pay a lot of attention. You like your birthdays because all of your friends remember you and you get cards and a party and maybe a free lunch. So these are yearly dramas: our parents' anniversary, our friends' birthdays, Thanksgiving, Christmas, Easter and every other God-forsaken holiday that we can't forget.

Then we consider miracles, which are even more distracting. Every once in a while something or some great number of things fall out of the sky, right in front of our eyes. Or maybe someone gets Enlightened for a week and knows all the answers to the koans. Great things happen. Someone gets healed overnight. We tend to pay so much attention to all these miracles and to all these problems we're having hourly, daily, weekly, monthly and yearly...

Then we have the problem called the Work, with a capital W, that I'm always talking about. Yet somewhere along the way, I think that we've lost the idea of happiness. It doesn't seem to Me that any of you are happy, unless of course you and I have a very different idea of what happiness is.

If you're going to attribute the kriyas, the mudras and the ecstasies to Me, you're going to have to attribute all the other mass of fuzziness as well. Because it's all just fuzzinesss so far, since I don't see anybody being happy. If I saw anybody being really happy, then I would say maybe we'd better look a little more deeply into the nature of our experience so we could radiate this happiness to others.

We're struggling so intensely that we forget that we're only pretending to be happy in moments in which we distract ourselves from the suffering underlying the struggle. Every once in a while we're sitting and meditating and all of a sudden this sorrow comes over us and we say, "Look at what I'm doing. It's all the Search. I'm always bitching and moaning and I never do my sadhana. Oh, what an awful thing it is." All of a sudden we remember we're not happy. We're supposed to be buzzing around and making preparations for puja and meditation and exercise and study and we have lots of things to prepare for to keep our minds distracted.

But none of this dilemma is necessary. It is possible to be happy—not to be in a good mood once in a while, to be exalted in the Presence of God only when we sing some holy chant—but to be really happy. And if we don't see that real happiness in ourselves, we should start to look at why.

It's not good enough to be distracted in miracles all the time, or any time at all. It's not good enough to think that the Work is so important that we can make everybody around us miserable—so long as we never forget our committment to the Work. It might be news, coming from Me, but there's something terribly wrong with the Work if that happens. There's either something terribly wrong with the Work, or something terribly wrong with us, every one of us.

I'll tell you, I think it's us. I've meditated on this for weeks without ceasing: waking, sleeping, dreaming and eating, without even so much as a second's release. And I think it's us. After lengthy and soul-baring deliberation, I think it's us. I think that if simply being in the Presence of the undoubtedly Divinely Influential Spiritual Master for four years still allows us this unhappiness every day, we'd better start looking at what's going on. Seriously; this is not a lark. We'd better start looking at it as if our lives depended on it (which they do).

There is hope, however. We all like hope; it's inspiring. But there is a problem with that. So long as there's hope, there's also hopelessness. After all, what good are miracles if we're not happy? Four years is enough. It's not a lark. It's not a lark for Me. It's about time we take a good look at what's going on.

Consider this: you can never take back anything you've ever said or done. You can see that in action when you say something in front of your children. Anything. I thank the Lord I've only sworn two oaths in my entire life because you can't take back anything that you say, ever. This alone should give you grave cause for concern, as long as you continue to function in a conventional way. There is a possibility for you not to feel terrible about this, and guilty and awful and hopeless and everything else. But as long as you continue to function automatically and blindly in a conventional way, then you should, in fact, feel really hopeless, because you (all of us) are always doing and saying things that are enough to traumatize everyone in your environment. But don't lose faith because everybody in your environment is so insensitive they don't get it anyway. It registers on their brains and makes an impression in memory, but that's all. Most people don't have the good sense to be conscious.

I'm plenty worried. Can you imagine that I can keep my sense of humor in the midst of this? I am making jokes but I am serious at the same time. I'm worried, but I'm not worried for Me. I'm a stoic. You live, you die, it's no big deal. I'm not worried for Me. I can live and die heroically, stoically and it'll be okay. I'm really worried for you. If that seems to contradict the rhetoric, don't feel bad. It's not Me I'm suffering, I'm suffering the illusory one.

The one that's suffering is totally an illusion. There's nothing real about your unhappiness. Genuinely and truly I guarantee you there's nothing real about your unhappiness. You feel it, beyond a doubt. You emote it, you think it. That's certainly real. But the genuineness of your unhappiness is not to be found anywhere. All we can find is the reflection of your unhappiness: your thinking, your emoting, your feeling. But the genuineness of your unhappiness is nowhere to be found.

So what are we going to do about the fact that we're suffering an illusion, and we refuse to give up the illusion? And what am I going to do about the fact that I see you being occasionally ecstatic, getting a glance from Me and melting right there into the floor? It is true that I sometimes recognize a light in your eyes that is absolutely brillant—but despite all that, here we are. It seems that I* am making you ecstatic, and that I am making you absolutely miserable.

The last thing Neem Karoli Baba said before he died was, "What am I going to do? Nobody understands me." I'll be damned if that's going to happen to Me. It's not going to happen. I don't know what to *do* about it, though, since I'm not making you work. We have quite a dilemma here, if you ask Me. You don't think we have a dilemma because I make you laugh and there are ecstasies once in a while and you're always having lessons made in your lives.

How can you complain if you're always having lessons made in your lives? What more could you ask for? You're always learning things. I'm always exhorting you to follow the conditions and since you don't do them perfectly, that makes you feel good because I'm always giving you so much attention in my exhortations.

And I'm always forgiving you. You don't know that, do you? Have I ever said face to face to any of you, "I forgive you?" How do you *know* I forgive you? You think this is Christianity? I might be going around cursing you. You think this all-compassionate Lord is so forgiving? Because I don't open my mouth, you think I'm always so forgiving? Hah! But, then again, maybe I am. It's possible that I do forgive you for all your sins. Just possible.

Tonight, here we sit, laughing and enjoying ourselves, but don't forget, we're in deep trouble. Just imagine that everything that has ever happened in your environment can never be erased. We shouldn't be trying to get better, under any circumstances. It's a totally useless process. We couldn't redo one percent of all the garbage that's in our chemistry. If we worked our whole lives, we might be a little clean, we might develop manners...well, maybe it wouldn't be so bad to have that kind of community. We could use some manners. But that's another story.

Consider what would happen if we were Alive. Everything we've invested our whole lives in would be invalidated. We've got a lot of considerations since everything that's ever been said in our environment is working and gurgling and bubbling, doing its dance of the seven veils. You know, all those nasties that our mommies and daddies and friends said...to try to redo all that business is a hopeless case. But we are trying to understand spiritual life within the given perimeters or parameters of our previous education. It's an impossibility.

Some of us have a relatively good handle on it. We can rap that dharma out and give impressive seminars. But basically, we're not happy. I see some very bright eyes, some incredible ecstasies, but we're not *happy*. Unless, of course, your idea of being happy is different than Mine. My idea of being happy...let me tell you what it is not. It's not being so committed to the Work, whatever the hell that is, that everybody in the environment is miserable as a result of your intensity.

The Work, as far as I'm concerned, you can throw the Work out the window if you're not happy. You're not supposed to plod through life gnashing your teeth. The Work isn't supposed to be *work*. It's supposed to be Suffering, not suffering. Conscious suffering is not suffering as you understand the word.

Something is terribly wrong. We shouldn't even be talking about the Work if we aren't happy in one another's company. It doesn't matter if someone breaks a plate or a glass with our monogram on it. Whatever we hold precious, it doesn't matter. If we cannot be happy in one another's company, regardless of what goes on, the Work doesn't mean a thing.

You come home and find your dog lying dead on his side with his legs stiff and his tongue hanging out. I'm sure that would create a lot of sorrow but it doesn't mean you have to not be happy. What does that have to do with happiness? What does our territory have to do with happiness? If someone puts his foot into your territory, we have border clashes. So what? What does that have to do with being happy? It doesn't have anything to do with being happy because when you make *that* have something to do with being happy, you cannot be happy.

You're never going to redo all the head, body, emotion stuff. Every word ever said in anger in every fight you've ever had; you're never going to redo all that stuff. Not ever. Not if you had an eternity to do it. Because you're not going to stop having fights. Even in the midst of being happy, you're not going to stop having fights. Some day you're going to have a fight and say something you are sorry for and you're not going to be able to take it back, ever. So you've got to Be Different.

You can't do all of this stuff over. You can not do it. You absolutely cannot do all the tears over. Can't do all the happy times over, either. You can't do it. You can take that picture of your baby, when he or she was six months old and look at it from now 'til doomsday, but your baby will never be six months old again. I can promise you, you aren't going to be able to redo the happiness that child gave you when that picture was taken, if you live for more years than you can count. You aren't going to redo those "good times." You're not going to redo the

Prom, the day you were Homecoming Queen, the day you hit that home run. You can't redo any of it. All you can do is *Be Different.* All you can do is be happy.

July 31, 1977

So, when we talk about sacrifice, it's not necessary to know what or who to sacrifice to. It's simply to serve the highest possible ideal and sacrifice to that, whatever it is. It doesn't mean to go out and immolate yourself, to do something dramatic like pouring gasoline over yourself and lighting a match. The idea of sacrifice is being in the most appropriate form for that which you are being used by. Reasons are all irrelevant because we'll never know who we're feeding or what we're being used for.

What's relevant is the law, which is sacrifice. The highest ideal mankind has is to serve God. Now sometimes that ideal has been somewhat trampled underfoot. Things have been done in the name of God that haven't been exactly kosher. Yet still, at the base of all of mankind's seeking is God. The highest ideal mankind has is God. And the object of all sadhana is to be perfect, not perfect with a limited concept of what perfect is (not a perfect yogi, or a perfect experience or perfect knowledge) just perfect for whatever it is we serve.

Sadhana. An awful word, isn't it? Sadhana. Couldn't they think of another word, something nice, like prune? Proon, prune—so smooth. Sadhana is a consciously intelligent process: recognizing under all circumstances that every single last event that arises in your life is an attempt to resolve your own inner conflict, when in fact, the whole conflict (or the whole delusion of the conflict) arises because you choose to ignore and deny the already present and eternally true union. In fact, there is no such thing as union. What is there to be united with? There is no conflict, there is no separation, there is nothing but God. Maybe there's not even God. That would be a kick in the ass wouldn't it?

You get to the pearly gates, and you see St. Peter and you say, "Hey, I'm finally going to see God."

St. Peter shakes his head and says to you, "Well, I hate to disappoint you but there is no God."

"But these are the pearly gates and you're St. Peter."

"Yeah, I know, but there's no God, man."

"But what's behind those gates?"

When you walk through, you see this enormous factory. You don't get wings and a white robe. You get dirty old khaki pants and a dirty old khaki shirt. Everyone, male and female. You look just like some guerilla army—sweaty and smelly. And you get to work in this factory for eternity. So you seek out St. Peter. "I want to go to the other place."

"There is no other place."

"Huh?"

"Yup. That's the way it is."

So St. Peter tells you that if you work in the factory for eternity, you're going to come to realize sooner or later that nothing ever changes. It's all the same. And it's all perfect because this is just the way it is.

We think that we're going to be transported into realms of infinite variety in taste and delight and experience. No, we're not. Maybe one of you will make it to one of those realms. You'll careen off the wave you're travelling on and hit one of those realms.

There are three phenomenal realms that you get a chance to ricochet off of by accident. One is the loka of Ultra-Bright. It's very nice there; nobody has any lips. Fluoridation is spontaneous and God-present, so you never have to brush your teeth.

The second is the Brylcream loka. You get a chance to get squeezed out of a tube by someone of the opposite sex. And your hair is never greasy.

Then there's the Shake 'n' Bake loka, which is even better. The only problem is that people don't last long there. They have these big chickens that eat you. But that's to your advantage because you get to come back here, fast, as a chicken shit!

March 1, 1983

I would recommend that you begin to allow Divine Influence to manifest in your life the way it needs to manifest, to purify you in a certain way. How many of you have felt like skipping and jumping and singing and falling on the grass on a sunny day and you haven't done it? If you are at all sensitive, that is very painful because it's just like being bound in a staitjacket. On the basis of my own experience, I can suggest this: it is really not worth being contained, cramped in that way.

There is only one reason why you don't move in the way you feel. You are worried about what other people think. You subscribe to a dharma that prescribes the agony of separation from God. You subscribe to the idea that the world, which is all that is not God, is not worth a plug nickel and yet you refuse to be ecstatic in God because of the very thing you have ascribed as being totally worthless. Isn't that ridiculous? Anyone you have ever been embarrassed in front of, because of—what do *any* of those people mean to you right now? What control do they have over your life? None, whatsoever, yes?

Think of all the people you've dehumanized yourself for. What do they mean to you? You have no tangible obstruction in the body. Why are you not happy?

Neurosis is not a form of energy. Pride, envy, greed, they are not real. They have no substance. They are zero, void. But you allow them to make the body tight, impure, full of toxins. They crystallize muscles in obstructive ways. And still you indulge them, unreal as they are; they still create pain.

You must Enquire of the nature of this work if you are not happy. Nothing stands in the way of your being happy. Those things just appear tangible; they are only to the degree you are willing to make the false real.

When you understand *life,* you are called to *live.* When you understand the whole "program" that you are, just that realization is enough to make you want to fall down at my feet, to radiate the glory of God.

When you realize the life you are called to leave behind, that instant is Prayer. Since I am dedicated to your submission to God, to your own Happiness, I will continue to remind you of the fullness of a Divinely Influenced, brilliantly clear life. To Realize Me is to Pray. I have been sacrificed for you and I wait.

Frog

February 21, 1984

Lee: Jesus was a dancer, Buddha was a sculptor, Krishna was a rogue. And they're all this One. *(He's reading from a slip of paper.)* Let's see, what can I make of that?
Student *(an editor)*: Where did you get that?
Lee: Huh? *(He looks at the questioner incredulously as if to say "Why don't you realize I came up with this stuff when it's this good, you shit." The room explodes in laughter. Students are screaming and clapping and going wild.)*
Another student: Yeah, where *do* you get your material?
Lee: There, you see what I mean. I put those words in his mouth a half hour ago. *(referring to Divinely setting up all manifestations to produce God Realization, the profound ease and delight present in the room all night being indicative of the way it should always be.)*

You think you know what you say and that you think uniquely and independently. I put the words in your mouth and I put the gestures in your body. I've designed the whole thing. This evening was scripted. Everything that has gone on since we walked into this room, since the chanting ended, was scripted. How could it have been more perfect for what we're looking for?

That's what this is, *The Living God Blues.*

(Student makes a gurgling soul sound.)
Lee: What was that? *(laughter)* Who was that gurgling man? Who was that gurgling man that left that glob of phlem on the floor? Hi-ho slobber away!

There's a vast and popular movement in Christianity today to make Jesus some heavy obsessed character. What a dull, sad, old man he must have been if he was what these people imagine. Trudging with intention toward his crucifixion. *(in a very serious tone)* Knowing that he only had three years to teach, and that he was going to sacrifice his life for the sins of the world. What a drudge. What an awful thing to lay on a guy who was a *dancer.*

Jesus was a dancer. He loved the sun, the land, the breeze, the "common" people. That's why he was in Galilee. That's why he went out to the desert. He went out and breathed the sun and danced. He wasn't a methodical, dull character, heavied out by the knowledge that he was going to die with stakes through his hands and stakes through his feet. He was a dancer. He whirled and twirled and leaped through his ministry. But people have made him to be this character who was burdened by a profound knowledge that he was sacrificing in an exclusive way, that he was the *only* begotten Son of God. What a stigma (no pun intended) to lay on somebody! The *only* begotten Son of God and there would never be another; he was going to leave the world empty of the possibility of *ever* having the Son of God live again. What a ridiculous concept and consideration—that millions of people are buying today, hook, line and sinker.

Jesus was a dancer who realized that he *was* the Son of God and that the Son of God would continue to manifest whenever the dance was needed.

He danced through his ministry. He dazzled people. Imagine these two fishermen, standing on the shore, casting in their nets, and this guy comes along *(the Master put on a dreary voice)* with his shoulders bent, trudging along the sea. He says, "Follow me *(in a sad and dejected voice)* you guys. I'm going to die first and then you're going to be martyrs, but the world needs you, so you'd better follow me."

Hey man! They were pulling in empty nets and they were a little bummed out because they made their living fishing and there were no fish today. Here comes this genie, tripping along the sand, sparkling light from his toes and floating above the ground and they are bowled over. This guy whips around and does a routine, a schtick, and they are in awe. These two fishermen had never seen anything like it. And then he says, "Follow me" with a delight and a joy they had never dreamed of. Vaudeville. And they reply, "We'd like to, *(sigh)* but, but, but..." So Jesus says, "Throw your nets in" and they do as he bids. They pull them out full of fish. And he says, "You guys thought women were fun. Get a load of this bass!"

How could they help but be intrigued? "If you could make a cold, clammy bass feel like this *(Lee shouts)* then lead on, brother, lead on."

That's what Jesus did. He *lived.* He was wild. When he told people to follow him, they were dazzled by his act. He didn't come along and promise them martyrdom. He was a dancer. He twirled through his ministry. Everywhere he went he drew crowds. They came to watch him dance. They didn't come to hear heavy spiritual raps about sin and guilt. They came to watch him dance and when he danced, it made them think that their burdens weren't all what they had assumed them to be. Jesus woke people up when he danced.

Buddha was a sculptor. He was cool. Buddha worked slowly, gradually, retiringly. Jesus was a man of the people. He drew crowds; he had a flair. Buddha was a different kind of artist. A sculptor works alone in his studio. Working long and hard and gradually molding a piece. He wasn't a dazzler, he sculpted. People listened to what he had to say, followed the Teaching, developed vast monasteries and convents during his lifetime, but it was a slow process of sculpting. It wasn't dazzling. It was very methodical and slow. But the final outcome? A work of art.

Krishna was simply a rogue. He was a rogue lover, a rogue warrior, a rogue king. When he was a child, he was mischievous. He loved to play practical jokes on people.

There was a time in which his mama caught him with his hand in the butter pot, eating all the butter. She said, "This time I'm going to fix you." So she took a rope out and tried to tie him up and everytime she tried to tie him up, the rope was never long enough. She kept getting longer and longer and longer lengths of rope. She was getting more and more frustrated and he would just look at her with that twinkle in his eye. He seduced her. He seduced his mother time and time again. He seduced his friends. He seduced women when he got older. He seduced men when he was a warrior. He seduced Arjuna. He was a rogue.

And *I* am all three—a dancer, a sculptor and a rogue *(pause)* and *then* some.

Any other questions?

A student in the back: I got it.

Lee: Great. *(And then he dictates as if he were reading)* The spiritual Master, in his profound compassion, hears one of his devotees say, "I got it" and assumed he did. So be it.

November 4, 1981

When *Spiritual Slavery* was written, we were all innocents, and yet now, after nine years, we find that the most mundane involvement is slavery to God and fulfillment of the Law. Slavery to the Law of Sacrifice is just slavery to the Law. Spiritual Slavery, (which we used in the early days in a very naive way, and improperly) actually refers to the slavery that one engages with the utmost rapture of Loving God. Slavery to the Law, which is the least consideration of this Way, is fulfilling the Will of God. Slavery to the Law is just the beginning, yet it is also the culmination of the process of submission to the Great Process of Divine Evolution.

The Gift of God is Loving God. So Spiritual Slavery is Loving God, Loving God subsumingly, not merely in your body or in your emotions. When you really Love God, you are a slave to God's Whim, not God's Will. The essence of God's Will is the Great Process of Divine Evolution. The Heart of God is Whim.

To follow the Will of God is to appropriately fulfill the Law of God in every moment. The Will of God is the gradual process of evolution that surrenders itself to the next moment of evolution. If we are fulfilling the Law of Sacrifice, not only in a mystical sense but for the next generation, that is Sacrifice. If you sacrifice to the Law, you surrender to the Will of God.

A Lover of God is a slave to the *Whim* of God. The Whim of God rests on the fulfillment of the Law in any moment, but expresses itself in an a-Lawful way in any conceivable moment.

So you are called to madness. You are not called to be leaders of the world where you are rational and understand the Process. You are called to madness, but you want wisdom. Understand, though, that madness is not wisdom. To the Lover of God, even the consideration of wisdom is absurd.

Being a slave to the Will of God just happens if you *consider* Loving

God. Loving God is the *only* Gift. Serving humanity is just bullshit. Loving God and going mad is all that matters.

February 24, 1982

Student: It seems like there are times we can see who you are and there are times we are too close to see who you are. We become so jaded in your presence, we keep thinking of Lee the man who farts and tells crude jokes. How do we keep in mind who you are all the time?
Lee: There's the rub. Who am I?
Student: God.
Lee: No.
Student: Lee Lozowick.
Lee: No.
Student: Nothing.
Lee: No.
Student: Everything.
Lee: No. There's the rub.

(The Master picked up his cane, held it out toward the group and blew through it forcefully, turning from side to side as he did so to cover the whole Darshan Hall.) Then laughingly he said, "You can't possibly know who I am."

December 27, 1981

To be happy requires that "knowledge" be obviated by Love. You may possess a certain degree of knowledge in your interactions with others. But Loving God obscures even the most visionary experiences that relate to the Dharma. Now, these things may manifest in a Lover of God, but they manifest as sleep talk.

Did you ever go to camp where someone talks in his sleep? You ask them questions and they answer them and the next morning they don't remember it at all. A Lover of God may manifest all kinds of relationships, but the next day it is irrelevant. If you ask me a question, many times my answer is completely automatic. I don't think about it. It is sleep talk.

I used to see you all as glowing balls of light. Now all I see is every neurosis. I know too much to be happy. Here you are, the hope of the world. All of the great lineages in the next ten thousand, twenty thousand years are going to come from America. So here sits the future of mankind. And I look at you and all I see is wave after wave of inappropriateness. Look at the chips on your shoulders! And there is the future of mankind on top of all those chips!

You begin to see how much there is to do and how slowly the work goes. There is a breakthrough in someone and it seems so immense to them, but to me, I need a microscope to see it. I only see two dynamics: ego or the disposition of enlightenment. But it is my job and I will be quite responsible for it. One can't be happy with that knowledge, for it is too demanding.

There are some people who are serving the Teaching in holy ways. That is never enough. You can be the greatest Teacher on the face of the earth, and you are like a worm in the face of God. So you have to Love God. You must be drunk, blinded by the light of the Beloved.

May 29, 1984

Student: If you learn how to conserve your energy, how do you learn when to use it properly?
Lee: Everytime I talk to you, be it as a group or individually, *every time,* I tell you how to use that energy and what to do with it. When you have conserved energy to a certain point, you will remember what I've said to you and the answer will be obvious. I say something to you at a different level of awareness when you're listening to me. But it's getting in. When you reach the level of awareness at which I've said it to you, you will understand perfectly what I've told you. Level of awareness is the same thing as conservation of energy.

You've been getting the Teaching ever since you've been here. Manifesting the Teaching is a function of your own maturity. When you reach a certain level of maturity, you won't all of a sudden know the right questions to ask me. You'll realize you've already got the answers, because I haven't waited for the right questions to be asked. I've given you everything you need, already, time and time and time again. I've given it to you in fifty different ways, just in case you see, so that you'll get it at whatever level of awareness you hit. I've given it to you at all dimensions of your being, and I'm still giving it to you in all the arcs and planes and geometric forms, if you imagine your body as a three-dimensional image.

When you conserve energy to a certain point you will move into one of those dimensions as your reality, and the Teaching will become apparent to you. That's what you must know.

You don't have to worry about asking the right questions when you become intuitive or aware. When you become aware you will realize that I've already given you the answers to every important question you could ever ask.

December 2, 1979

It would be nice to end hunger in the world, but in a hundred years we'll all be dead anyway and so will all the people whose bellies we're supposed to be trying to fill. All of this is gonna go. All of this disappears sooner or later, the sun, the moon, the solar system. Our sun is dying. In several billion years the sun will be cold. Ultimately, all things die, planets, suns, solar systems.

But there *is* a level that is intangible (to the conventional training, but not to one who is "awake") that survives ultimately. That is the level on which we can work and on which our lives can rest. We don't have to be limited by this form, by the gross body and its obvious mortality. What is of ultimate value to me is that level that disregards and is untouched by the disintegration of a solar system or a universe. That's the level I'm talking about. That's the level I offer.

When somebody dives into this work with absolute faith, the form of his or her life might not appear to be ideal to family and friends. But the spiritual work that can result is ultimately valuable. The kind of work that can result from the psychological programs and therapies, all of the "centering" and the "balancing" and the humanitarian efforts that we might make are all temporary. Those "new age expressions of light" create good karma so that we can possibly get another chance at what we are being offered now, here, but they don't create the kind of ultimate spiritual work that's absolutely necessary, that's ultimately necessary. That's what I'm interested in.

March 14, 1984

At a certain point of maturity, reactivity is a luxury you can ill afford. Reactivity then becomes a sickness. You need to seriously consider that reactivity to anything that arises in this Work is a luxury. The more mature you become in this Work, the poorer you become. One would think you would become richer as you progress, but you don't. You become poor in spirit, as the man said.

The Will of God is the movement towards the Disposition of Enlightenment, toward the clarity that is expressed in freedom, in all of you. What is it that moves you towards the Disposition of Enlightenment? It's the work that's provided here in the interaction with Divine Influence. If there's reactivity to that, which is the Will of God, it gives you a sense of the nature of what we're involved with here. So don't take yourself too seriously. If all you ever do is see the dark side of things, that's very significant in terms of your sadhana. It's a check point along the way. It tells you that you're sniffin' up the wrong tree. It's very simple.

Reactivity is a luxury we can ill afford. For some of you, it's a luxury which should never be present anymore. Your work has progressed too far. You're moving too quickly. At the level on which we're now working, reactivity is like a noose around someone's neck. Reactivity is the hangman and the noose is around the neck of the Work. If you display a certain amount of reactivity, the Work is strangled, choked to death.

People come here quite wealthy, with many luxuries: pride, vanity, prejudice, anger, competitiveness and reputation. Some poeple come to the Work with reputation as a function of the college they went to or the town that they grew up in or the family name. Whatever it is, it's a luxury. We have come to this work wealthy beyond most people's imaginations. Yet the longer we're here, the more we get stripped of our wealth. We end up poor, but Real.

That's what Jesus meant by, "It's harder for a wealthy man to enter the kingdom of heaven than for a camel to fit through the eye of a needle." That's what he meant by wealthy, although conventionally it's taken to mean money. A wealthy man is a man who can afford all the luxuries of ego, the excesses of personality. That's wealth. You stay here long enough, you become poor and happy. Poor and Real and happy. You can't be happy if you're wealthy. You can only be happy when you're poor.

What do you have to protect when you're poor? If you aren't busy protecting, the energy that you free up is mind boggling. What does that energy do when it's freed up? It ascends. The energy is usually held in the lower three centers where greed and avarice and the drive to power and control are. They're held there by the energy, literally, and when that energy is freed, it rises just like heat. That's how the higher centers mature. The higher centers don't mature by perfecting greed and avarice and power. The higher centers are fed by the dissolution of the energy that's held in the lower centers. So when you breathe, instead of all the food that's taken in by the breath being lost below your navel, if there's nothing to hold it there, it ascends. There you have it, in a nutshell.

The more reactivity you have, the less you're willing to accept My communication, the more resilient I become. The more you're willing to accept My communication, the more fragile I become. At a certain level, the fragility is such that if you drag out one of the luxuries, like reactivity, from the closet, it's like throwing a bomb in the middle of the room. I'm more affected now than I was, even two years ago. Years ago there was very little chance of doing a certain kind of work. Now I'm more vulnerable. I've put myself in a position of vulnerability, because of the crucial nature of this work *having to be done.* It *has* to be done, or the world dies.

Those are the facts, ma'am, nothing but the facts.

I give my life to the Community so that the community draws something from Me. And as the community draws something from Me, I draw something from you. So I begin to manifest more of people's conditioned dispositions as they begin to manifest more of My disposition. This is a reciprocal feeding process.

You're beginning to take on more responsibility and the taking of that responsibility is a sign of maturity. It requires more of you to do this Work, now. You only get what you avail yourself of. I've got a lot of secrets still. If you avail yourself of more, you receive more. That's why it took eight years for Assertion to be explained.

When I say reactivity affects Me, I'm not talking about an ordinary thing where you want to help your child or you want to help your parents or you want to help your friends. I'm talking about your ticket out of here.

You must want to keep Me around. You don't want to keep Me around because I'm your buddy or anything like that. That may be in your vision, but you should want to keep Me around because I'm your ticket to Paradise. I'm your ticket to heights undreamed of: I'm your ticket to lunch! A free ticket! That's why you should want to maintain a certain space for Me. You should want to keep Me here until you avail yourself of everything I have to give you. You don't want to let Me go down with secrets. You want to keep Me here until you have the maturity to avail yourself of *everything* I have to give you. And then, when I've given you everything I have to give you and you've digested it, then I can become an icon. Once every secret I have to give has been given, I serve no function, except as a figure head. I'll be royalty.

Rooster

February 22, 1984

Lee: Okay gang, inspire me.

Student: It seems as if there are two types of sadhana. First, there's the way of having everything built up, the tension builds, you're cornered and then you drop it, and there seems to be another way which is somehow just removing the mask. So my question is, is it possible just to remove the mask?

Lee: That's just what I was going to talk about tonight, except I was going to talk about it in the sense that we're all wearing hats rather than masks. And the hats we're all wearing have two eyes, one nose, two ears, lips, teeth, hair under the arms and in all our various cracks and nooks and crannies, toes, fingernails, nipples, breasts and various projections and indentations and so on. Hats are pretty neat. Most of you have recognized the extraordinary difference it makes in someone when they put on a hat. Have you noticed that?

The right hat makes you like a different person. It completely changes one's force, and to vary the hat, completely varies the communication.

We're all like that. We're all just wearing hats. The problem is we think we are the hat. So really there is only one way in sadhana.

Actually if you consider the whole process of building up and building up and release, what do you get when there's a release? You get a new hat, right?

Student: You get a free moment...

Lee: Well, you get a moment that feels free in contrast to the moment in which there was tension. But both moments are in the context of identification as a hat. You just put a different hat on.

Student: But doesn't that deny the whole principle of shock as a tool to "wake one up" for a bit, or throw one into a higher level?

Actually, shock is not designed to relieve tension, it's designed to clarify identification. If shock is ideally implemented, what it will effect is the separation of the identification of who *you* are with the hat.

It won't change your state within that identification.

Student: That's the same thing as taking off the hat a little bit?

Lee: Right. If you can recognize that you're wearing a hat, you can also recognize who it is that's wearing the hat. The only way you can recognize that is to disassociate from the identification as the hat. It's very difficult because the association is not an intellectual association. The mind, body, the emotions believe that they are the hat. So all changes in state, even wild shifts into mystical realms, are at best changing hats.

We even recognize that a change of role is like putting on a different hat. So there's only one thing to do, which is to disidentify with our belief that we are the hat, by resting in the root of consciousness that is prior to the inception of that identification. That is the only thing to do.

Student: Is that a discipline?

Lee: No, but discipline is required. That is not a discipline, but discipline is required.

With discipline, you come to recognize that even though there are vast changes in state, there are no changes in essence. Without discipline, you don't come to realize that except in random moments. But not with the kind of strength and dynamism that you recognize it with if you have discipline.

Student: What exactly happens? It feels like ego is a force and a power and it's got more power than essence.

Lee: Ego is a force and a power that mistakenly identifies itself as a thing.

Student: Something solid?

Lee: Something solid. Ego believes it is *this. (Lee sweeps his arm to indicate the material surroundings.)* Not what this really is, but...ego believes it is the physical body along with its compliment of feelings, emotions and thoughts.

Student: And ego isn't any of that?

Lee: No, it's a process that believes itself to be a something. But actually ego is a nothing. It's a nothing. I mean it's not even like air. It's not even like space. It's a nothing, absolutely! It's an absolute nothing! Nothing. The minute the misidentification stops, the process stops. You are something...but not what you think you are. And when you can cease the illusion of identification, ego is immediately nothing because it is nothing already anyway. See if you cease the misidentification, the illusion of identification...

Student: ...with thinking that ego is something...

Lee: No, with believing that you *are* the hat, there is no ego left to deal with because it's nothing.

Student: So what's left?

Lee: What's left is what is real.
Student: Out there?
Lee: There is no out there or in here. What's Real is what's Real.
Student: ...the image of "prior than," the whole image that we're given is that you're prior to all of that illusion. How does that figure in this?
Lee: There is a point of inception. There is a point in the movement of things, in the physics of things at which that identification is made. And the point at which the identification is made is the point at which we cease to be awake. The problem that dharmically arises is, what's the difference between us and a toad? Or us and this piece of wood? This piece of wood does not identify itself as this piece of wood. It's simply conscious. Toads have no hopes and dreams. They don't project into the future and they don't remember the past. When there's toad picnics, they don't get together and swap stories about when they were tadpoles.

"Oh God, I remember when I was a tadpole, shit man. I mean I was in a pond and there was so much algae. God, it was fantastic. I would pig out everyday." They don't do that. They don't remember when they were tadpoles. They don't get together and say, "Yeah, I'm looking forward to old age. You know, schtuppin' a few of the women toads. It's a hell of a thing being able to have two hundred babies. Shit, man. My old toad had two thousand eight hundred eggs last year. Shit man."

They have no projection into the future, nor remembrance of the past. They're just present as consciousness. On the other hand, they're not aware that they're present as consciousness. And the unique configuration of chemistry represented within the dimension of light that we are as human beings, gives us the ability to be conscious, consciously. Not just to be consciousness. To be conscious.

So there is a point in the physics of things in which we assume identification with this. Which is like being a toad. We are already presently Enlightened. So even in our sleep we are not unenlightened.
Student: Because ego is an illusion anyway?
Lee: Right. Well, because ego is an illusion and what that means is, if you follow that argument, as dense a human being as could exist, is consciousness. The difference is, we have the capacity to be conscious, in fact it is our destiny to be conscious, not just consciousness. It is our born destiny to be conscious.
Student: Of consciousness?
Lee: Well, not *of* anything. Just conscious. If you are conscious, you're not conscious *of* anything, including consciousness. You're just conscious. But that's different than being consciousness. Which is not conscious. Being consciousness, you're simply a part of the physics of things.

Student: Like a yogi or something?

Lee: No, like a tadpole or a toad. Being conscious you *are* the physics of things. Being conscious, you make the sun rise in the morning. You make the earth spin on its axis. You make the stars explode and regenerate and be born. You are literally THE creator when you are conscious. When you are consciousness, you are simply a part of the ongoing physics of things.

Student: That's why in *Beyond Release* you said, "I am the world. I'm just claiming my heritage."

Lee: Exactly. That's why I said the other night that whatever I say is real, despite facts that might contradict that. Whatever I say is real. If I say that right now it's the middle of the day and there are no walls here and we're sitting in the middle of a glorious field, that's exactly what is real. And you say, "What's the guru trying to do? He's trying to be paradoxical. Obviously there are walls here and we're sitting in the Darshan Hall."

No we're not. You should never allow the facts to interfere with what is real.

We could come up with volumes of scientific proof to substantiate your belief that you are sitting in a room, on a floor, covered by an indoor/outdoor carpet of a sort of nauseous green color, staring up at an exquisitely designed chair of black walnut, upholstered in raw silk with a guru sitting up there, but you're not. There's no one sitting up here, there's no chair; we're in a field. The sky is cloudless above us. The sun is shining. There are daisies and buttercups and violets all around. That's the truth of things. There's *no* other truth, despite the imposition of what your senses tell you. The imposition of what your senses tell you is simply what your senses tell you. There's no truth to it. Do you follow? Do you believe me? *(The group acknowledges with a loud "yes." And immediately Lee remarks)* No you don't. How can you believe me? Your senses are screaming with the pressure of your cramp. Your senses are being shattered by the feeling *(the group is laughing uncontrollably)* of bright blue zafus pressing your tight buttocks. Talk about inelegance: bright blue zafus on a dark green indoor/outdoor carpet is really the pits. I don't think we could have picked a worse color scheme. Anyway...

It's nice that you say you believe me; and you want to believe me because you intuit what I'm saying and you've actually had biological experience, or organically Innocent experience of what I'm saying but you can't *believe* me. Because you're under the assumption that you're this *hat.* A hat with eyes and a nose and ears and so on.

Wouldn't it be great if hair grew under breasts? I mean why shouldn't it? It grows under arms. It grows between legs. Why wouldn't hair grow under breasts? Why doesn't it just grow under breasts? Not all over, just under. And if you lifted them up, there it would be. *(laughter)* Isn't hair meant to be sexually enticing anyway? Aren't we supposed to procreate the species because women have hair under their arms and men have hair on their chests and genitals are covered with hair? Why isn't there hair under breasts? Isn't that attractive? What are all men attracted to but breasts. Men are barely attracted to vaginas compared to their attraction to breasts.

When guys are in high school and they want to rank out women they say, "Turn them upside down; they all look the same." They talk about how women's vaginas smell. But they never talk about breasts like that. Breasts are sacred. *(laughter)*

We grew up sucking breasts and if we didn't we wanted to. Then we spend the rest of our lives trying to recreate the first two years of our lives where we didn't. Why isn't there hair under breasts? Why is there hair on vulvas? I don't understand it. Can somebody explain that to me?

(Lee waits a few seconds.) No, of course not. Because there's no reason. So don't try. But you would do well to explain it to yourself. Particularly the men. Then you'd stop feeling the way you feel about vaginas. Except that they're... Vaginas. God, who ever made up that word? Vaginas. Talk about something that doesn't sound like what it is. *(sigh)*

September 8, 1982

The principle of this Way is not essentially one of form; not principally a consideration of what we eat, where we live, what we wear, and so on. It is primarily a recognition of this: can we *consider* Loving God in an active, bodily way? The essence of this Way is about surrender to the Will of God in the midst of the consideration of Loving God. Surrender to the Will of God is the foundation of a True spiritual culture. Surrender to the Will of God is submission to the Great Process of Divine Evolution, allowing moment to moment functioning from a disposition of Enlightenment.

In the midst of the purification naturally encouraged by the demand to surrender to the Will of God and by the ongoing process of sympathy to that, one must *consider* Loving God through bodily, emotional and mental relationship to, and care and love and compassion and consideration for, one another.

The physical situations of our lives may very well vary immensely, may become more comfortable, or more trying, but none of that is more than incidental. Your focus must cease to be the content of your search for release and desire-fulfillment, and must become the active consideration of Loving God. You must persist under all conditional changes *if* you are to live this Way with the bliss of present happiness and ease.

November 1, 1981

I was thinking about how incredibly damnable our search for comfort is. When you are cold, and I don't mean freezing, you are obsessed with the fact that you are cold and how that obsession obscures your search for God. I was thinking about how some of you ask about ways of intentionally juicing your sadhana. If you want to begin in a little way which is attractive to God, sustain discomfort for yourself. I am talking about mild discomfort, not extreme austerities. Just in the span of your day, when it catches you, you can work with it.

If you find yourself a little bit cold or a little bit hot, don't go to remedy the situation right away. If you allow yourself a little discomfort, that's an attraction to God. You can either put on a sweater or you can consider Loving God. The consideration of Loving God can obscure everything else. So when you are cold, you can think about Loving God or you can immediately remedy the discomfort.

There is physical discomfort, such as being hot or cold, emotional discomfort, such as feeling lustful or angry and so on; and mental discomfort, such as watching a movie which is very gory or having prejudice of or abhorance to certain things.

All of the spiritual Masters have spoken about suffering. One of the things that attracts God is suffering. Why do you want to attract God? The only Grace is Loving God. God will Gift you with Loving God randomly, but also there is an attraction. If God is not attracted to you, there is no chance of getting Gift.

Two approaches attract God. One is suffering and the other is devotion, obedience and surrender. Since you can't intentionally be devotional or surrendered, the easiest thing to do is to create a situation where there is mild suffering. Like herpes. "The only Gift is herpes." It is spontaneous, eternal and creates all three: physical, emotional and mental suffering. What an advantage!

November 30, 1982

Student: Sometimes what arises is rage. You are much less likely to choose to work with a cramp when you are in a rage than when you are a little depressed. The pain arises from an attitude I am being forced to look at, and it starts to become a huge distraction rather than being used. It is so difficult to use pain. And yet, in the midst of pain, there is a slim chance that you are going to want to use that pain.
Lee: Yes, there is a chance. Sooner or later, you hear the Teaching. Until the shift comes, you think about it and reflect on it after it happens.
Student: That's very frustrating. You could spend *years* here without hearing the Teaching.
Lee: Yes, of course, that is one alternative, but only one of many. You can hear the same thing over and over again, but each time you hear it, you hear it on a different level. Now you've heard the Teaching to the degree that you are willing to question the whole process, at least. One of the ways you use pain is after it has subsided, allow it to push you toward piercing the cramp, allow the frustration it creates to be a "goad to God." If you didn't have this pain, you would never be moved to ask this question, you see?
Student: And yet there seems to be a big difference between the state I am in now and what you do in the midst of pain. Why is pain necessary?
Lee: The only reason it is necessary is to make you pierce the cramp. The only real value is to turn you in upon it to make you realize why it's there, how it is quite unnecessary, an illusion really.
Student: It's frustrating because I haven't done it yet.
Lee: It's just like an eternal circle. The same thing keeps happening over and over with more and more intensity until something breaks. It could go on for years, so you have to take a broader view of things. You say, "When it comes up, it's really powerful and unnecessary, but then it's gone in a few days" instead of "I wonder when it's going to come back, it was so awful."

So, if you can't stop that particular process, which you can't by any effort of will, then it's a matter of beginning to observe the root of the process itself. When you find yourself being negative, critical or gossipy, stop it right there through Enquiry or Obedience.

Student: That's walking away from the way I've lived for twenty-five years.

Lee: That's what you are doing here. The radical nature of our life is to walk away from everything we've invested in for twenty-five years because all of that is our trash, our feces, eh? People come here and attempt to set up what they have always done, but with a spiritual flavor, a little new-age twist, and it doesn't work.

It seems to you just now that this problem is unsolveable, and yet everybody has to pierce the same cramp. Your born disposition is never going to change. You are never going to be cool, distant, philosophical. You have to be responsible for that. Your disposition is a feeling disposition. Some people will have their existential crisis in their heads, but you experience the crisis in your body.

Student: So no matter where you feel the pain, you always think it's worse than another kind of pain, than someone elses?

Lee: Right.

Student: *(shaking her head)* It just doesn't seem fair.

Lee: All right, I'll confess. It's true, *you're* right, we are all conspiring to get you. *(wild laughter)*

Student: This could go on for twenty lifetimes!

Lee: That's true, or twenty thousand lifetimes. Okay, let's make a deal. When you get to be sixty, if you haven't changed, I'll give you all the fancy yogic techniques, so at least you'll salvage this lifetime with a little good karma.

Student: Bo. *(a nonsense syllable yelled out as a shakti manifestion)*

Lee: Okay, fifty-five.

Do you remember the story about two devotees of Krishna's? The first was a yogi who had spent his long life doing austerities. One day, Krishna appeared to him and the yogi asked Krishna when he would go to heaven.

In a hundred lifetimes," was Krishna's reply. The yogi became angry. "This is a bum deal," he exclaimed. "I'm sixty years old. I've been doing austerities all these years and now I have to wait."

"Tough luck," Krishna said as He walked off humming to Himself.

The second devotee was busy doing his practices when Krishna appeared to him.

"When will I come to be with you?" the devotee asked Him.

"In two million lifetimes," Krishna answered.

The man became ecstatic. "Is that all?" he cried and he fell at

Krishna's feet. In that moment he became merged into Krishna.

How many times have you read that story?

Student: Many times.

Lee: You have to begin to think differently, to be differently disposed. The minute you give into it, bing! You have a breakthrough. Make up your mind that when the pain comes, you will have a short but lousy time and then it will be gone, blasted away by the Light.

Student: But the real pain, the pain that causes the body to react, is always there. I can be happy and someone walks into the room and it's gone.

Lee: Because it's there all the time, you can't avoid it. You can only rest in the Primacy of Natural Ecstasy, prior to the pain. The pain is always there no matter what, as you say, unless it isn't there. This may sound inane but think about it. Or better yet, do it. Just live radiantly and blissfully, which is your natural condition prior to the inception of this pain. Just *do* it. Otherwise we will have this discussion again, don't 'cha know? The pain is your worldly legacy; it is the gift of the unrealized mind and the empty, sterile culture we are visiting for our seventy or eighty years. I offer you Happiness, the legacy of God. I offer you the *only* alternative to that pain which is a constant of the assumption of separation. I offer you the Lord, in all His splendor but the price is self-indulgence, unconsciousness, self-reference. In other words, it costs you that pain to live in My world. You must give it up, spend it completely. You have seen part of the picture quite clearly. Now, will you choose to be Happy? Will you choose to Realize your already perfect Enlightenment and *be* what that calls you to be? My parting question is, "Will you *do* it?"

June 28, 1983

It is common for spiritual students to dwell on their personal problems or cramps for long, long periods of time before coming to realize that an individual's "own" neuroses are almost irrelevant in the scheme of things. I would recommend that you consider this: every principle subsumes all other principles that serve less conscious or less true functions. The personal or isolated vision of ourselves as fragmented beings, separate from God and striving in individual ways to return to some kind of nebulous union or oneness with this God of our dreams, is a complete fallacy. We are already, always united, or more correctly, we are always already that which we think we must seek for. The laws of separation seem real, as does the attendant suffering. However, if we focus on, or become responsible for the laws of Realization or Enlightenment, regardless of how proficient we are at their fulfillment, all laws of separation cease to function, thereby allowing the machine of body and mind to slowly wind down, not in its necessary aspects, such as breath, digestion and so on, but in the unnecessary and fallacious aspects of its functioning, such as emotional recoil, the cramp of survival, and rest in the Primacy of God or Natural Ecstasy.

Community is the essential dynamic of human society. Community, Enlightened or true in its culture and activity, is the naturally Divine manifestation of the Great Process of Divine Evolution on earth. Community is the matrix for society. To cease to dramatize "my" problem and to consider "our" need, "our" demand and "our" activity as Community is to transcend entirely the reason for "my" problems to begin with. Why are "we" not activating Real Community? Consider "just this", and "my" problem is obviated, transcended in the intensity of the demand to solve "our" problem.

We need to provide a real culture. That is what is needed of Community. What's "our" demand? To communicate the Teaching through the Presence of Divine Influence and through the Benediction of my

Presence with you as Community. Not my physical attention to you as individuals, my Presence with you as Community. That will provide Benediction. My Presence with you as individuals does not communicate itself nearly as profoundly as my Presence with you as Community.

To consider what is "our" activity is to establish a holy and sacred environment in which people can find and can respond to "our" need and "our" demand. To consider that is to totally transcend the reasons for "my" problems to begin with.

The reason for "my" problems is that we really believe, on some primal level, that we are separate from God and that as individuals, we are eternal, that there is no such thing as union. We believe there is friendship, love, sexual union but there is not such thing as union. We see ourselves as isolated, independent events in the universe. And the degree of our isolation or the significance of our independence is our six feet, or five feet, six inches, one hundred and twenty pounds, whatever we are. That's what we believe. And the reason "I" have"my" problems is because of our belief system.

If we realized that Community is the essential manifestation of the Great Process of Divine Evolution, and that selflessness establishes the height of ecstasy—that you are happiest, genuinely happiest when you have the least concern for your own personal isolation...why would anyone not work toward making that a viable possibility?

So you have to begin to understand that "my" problems are because of certain reasons and you will cease to need those reasons if you consider "our" problem as Community. What's the need, what's the demand, what's the activity of Community? That's "our" problem. That's all.

Devote your life to Enlightened Community, not Enlightenment, which is just a part of "my" problem, and already perfectly true of everyone anyway. Devote your life to Enlightened Community with intense enthusiasm, passion and energy, and personal cramps or what have seemed to be personal obstacles, "my" problems and neurosis will automatically cease to manifest. They will just dry up and blow away in the wind. Raging jealousy, anger, frustration, envy, guilt, whatever it is, will dry up and blow away because it is founded on a completely illusory presumption. When the presumption shifts, everything that goes along with the illusion shifts, too. It disappears, all at once. You don't have to work your way through stacks and stacks of all that stuff. That's what I'm suggesting you consider.

If you are selfless, there is no self to be problematical. There is only an Enlightened, already happy man or woman who is surrendered to the Will of God and submitted thereby to the Great Process of Divine Evolution. Be selfless, and all of the delusions that you have accepted which have encouraged you to dramatize "my" problems will become transparent and will in turn not need "my" problems to substantiate them."My" problems will simply cease to arise.

"My" problems will simply cease to arise, being totally unnecessary and only a function of blindness and unconsciousness. Serve one another through the organic consideration of Loving God, and "our" problem becomes the universal Work of the Lord, our God, through the Divine Influence of the spiritual Master, which is itself the answer to all remaining questions which transcend themselves in the brilliance of the radiant love of selflessness.

"My" problem does not exist, and all work on "my" problem is completely useless, storing up karma but without a grain of spiritual value. If "my" problem does not exist, obviously working on it is simply absurd. "Our" problem as Community is the Work of God as man. "Just This" is the consideration I pose to you.

January 30, 1983

If you look around, if you open your eyes, life can really be quite a delight. There are times of tension, crisis, suffering, but if you were to keep a record of what was positive and what was negative, you would find that about ninety percent of your day is positive and only ten percent is negative.

Just getting up in the morning is a wonderful thing. But you forget. You open your eyes and think, "I'm going to see so-and-so at breakfast and she's going to be in one of her moods." And she isn't in that mood, yet you still have your negativity. Life is so incredibly vibrant. There is so much exciting mystery every day. So to think negatively, which is much too common, is to allow your whole life to be filtered through your negative attitude toward things. If someone bothers you, you may be annoyed in the moment, but when you leave them, you should cease to be bothered by that instead of hanging onto it.

When you think positively, you see what is and you respond to it in a flexible way. There are problems in life but your direct interaction with those problems takes up only a small portion of your day.

It may occur to you that even within the last year things seem to have gotten worse instead of better. That's because the negative thinking has become an habitual response. It's only more evident because it's become a stronger habit. And every time you indulge it, you reinforce it. Certain kinds of realizations become apparent because of sadhana. When you say, "Geez, this is awful" and you worry about it all day long, you develop a negative thinking habit. You are seeing things more clearly and because your tendency responds in a certain way, you develop a reaction to things.

The thing to do is to take a different relationship to what you see. What you see is what you see. You may see it, but you don't have to opinionate about it. Don't judge it. Don't get righteous about it. You have to intentionally and willfully turn your attention elsewhere.

In our school, you don't have to think of how to be positive. You assume that the Divine moves your life. That assumption should be tacitly obvious to you.

To think positively is to recognize the facts of things, positive and negative, without hanging onto them. In the morning when you get up, you should be charging around. You should be full of life. And most of you aren't.

In order to think positively, you have to know that you don't die. You must know there is a continuum, a continuity of life beyond the physical body. If you believe that when your body dies, you are going to be obliterated and that's it, you shouldn't be here. You should be out drinking and sexing. Why of all the beings on earth are *you* here? It's not chance.

You have to assume that you are Divinely influenced. You must intentionally bring that thought to mind. Many of you know you are not going to die, but still you persist in thinking negatively. Those two views make for tension and depression. You are always attempting to re-arm, to defend.

Negative thinking becomes more and more habitual and then it becomes chronic. Some of you know old people who are chronic negative thinkers and you may love them, but you don't want to be anywhere near them.

You are Divinely influenced. Divine Influence will not allow you to suffer anything that is unnecessary for you, for mankind, or for God. But a lot of the suffering that goes on now is unnecessary. That's not a matter of Divine Influence; it is entirely self-created.

There is only one way to change a pattern of negative thinking. You must act. What is action? An apology; a look; a touch; a word. Logical thought will never change an emotion. Action will. When you are jealous or angry don't sit and stew. Work, sing, go and say something nice to someone. Some people feel sorry for themselves and they sit down and stare at the walls. Go do something else!

May 3, 1984

There's an interesting dichotomy here. On the one hand, when "purification" is happening for you, analysis of it is essentially a waste of time. Then the body does things and you enter different states, to analyze why it is happening to you, what's going on, is senseless. It is all entirely subjective and it all passes.

When you're sick, you take care of yourself in a simple but healthy way and soon you're better. Go to bed if you have to, drink tea and get better.

On the other hand, we've seen something interesting happening for the last few years during the approach of our celebrations. The bigger the celebration, the more dramatic the phenomenon, it seems. A lot of people here seem to be going through significant "activity" in their bodies. Perhaps it's already in anticipation of Guru Purnima in July. Every celebration has been a step up for us these last nine years. Why not this one?

We've seen some major shifts of consciousness, we've moved into some exceptional spaces and there have been some really dramatic alterations in people's lives. We've been following that and recording that and interpreting that in our own way.

How long can we continue to make these kinds of breakthroughs? For how many years can the celebrations keep getting better and better? It seems as though that process can be almost endless. That is not the point, you see; far from it. Yet the natural way, when one is living from an Enlightened disposition, is that we mature, certainly, into the higher stages of life, but all transitions are subtle and easeful and natural. There aren't dramatic breakthroughs when you're living from an Enlightened disposition. You move through stages in a gentle and spontaneous way. You don't *have* any dramas.

So what's been happening here? People have shifted context. People have made significant movement into dimensions of appreciation of the maturity that wasn't present years ago. Yet the shifts that we've been making have to do with profound psychological transformation not spiritual transformation. What we're doing here needs to be done, to be sure. It will be done. The distinction is that if we mistake what we are doing for movement *towards* Enlightenment, then we're always tending to dramatize every bodily dynamic. We subconsciously verify our assumption that something is going on by getting sick. The sickness itself is virtually unnecessary. The phenomena (bodily reactions, severe swings of emotionality and such) are something we create because of the assumptions that we've made, because of the dynamic that we've habitually come to recognize, as *if* it were something other than what it is.

But the shift into an overall wisdom is something that perhaps we're still flirting with. There is a tremendous enticement—the next celebration!

The community head has seen people change and mature and "Wow, just think! The next celebration! Am I next?" or maybe "I've already had one shift, what's my next one going to be like?"

That's the old attitude of seeking that we began discussing nine years ago. If we were living from an Enlightened disposition, life would not be a matter of the build-up of enthusiasm towards a breakthrough, then a breakthrough, an adjustment, build up of enthusiasm towards a breakthrough, breakthrough, adjustment and so on. Celebrations would certainly be looked forward to with a certain amount of excitement, but for different reasons. Essentially, based from an Enlightened disposition, things would be much more consistent. Our lives would remain, for years on end the same: full of compassion, brilliance, delight, richness. There would be certain major celebrations that would be met with a greater enthusiasm, yet all would ultimately be the same.

We might have an idea of life, if we really stop to think about what our projection is, of just maturing through great leaps and dramatic breakthroughs, but that's not it. Those things are fine if they move us into spaces where we can begin to appreciate one another more and handle our work in a better way. But that's not it.

What it's about is a moment to moment genuine celebration in one another's company. That's a much more *even* kind of life, where our disposition remains essentially the same all the time: one of ease and gratitude and pleasure; where the changes of maturity that occur, just occur naturally and easefully in the context of our lives. We grow and we become wiser; we embrace more experience.

This is a crucial principle, that we don't mistake what we're doing as meaning we're getting closer to Enlightenment. You could easily make that mistake, because we're certainly making shifts of a significant nature. But I must caution you not to mistake what we're doing for getting closer to Enlightenment. We're not. We're no closer to Enlightenment now than when we began this work.

Enlightenment is already perfectly present. The movement into that assumption signifies the beginning of allowing the habit patterns that are chronic and conditioned to dissipate on their own, as they will, and to completely shift attitude.

We're *not* approaching Enlightenment, however. We are approaching a more significant state of human existence. That is the responsibility for what is already essentially true of us.

Cow

March 16, 1984

The Great Divine Milieu of Stodginess

There are those benefits that can be attributed to youth; the raw passions of the energy of exploration, and those benefits that can be said to be accrued in old age, the wisdom of experience, of a long life of observation and self-reflection, but there is a middle period, the profound and most far-reaching benefits of which can be said to be truly Greatly Divine. This is the period of stodginess.

One might think that stodgy people are dull and uninteresting, chronically trapped by patterns of habit and sloth. And one might assume that stodginess is a quality of all ages, but I must suggest that as we approach middle age, a certain funky and wildly (well, stodgily actually) "absent" mood sinks in which, if properly seen and reflected upon, can be the gateway to extraordinary Realization.

We are always so busy looking for our Enlightenment, actively pursuing self-observation, a disciplined mind, free and spontaneous Essential activity, and so on, all of which use great, great volumes of energy, all of which capture vast amounts of attention, that we don't really have enough energy or attention left to get right (hey, hey, a little dry humor there, eh what?). Actually, in point of fact, and for sure, (redundant?) it requires almost all of the energy and attention we can muster...Colonel Mustard, in the Den, oh, no, sorry, I just got distracted for a moment. Where was I? Well, here of course. Oh, how droll. Yes, so, it requires almost all of the energy and attention we can muster...Colonel—oh, no, caught you this time, you bugger—back on track, back, back you savage! Yes, so, actually it requires almost all of the energy and attention we can...we have access to (ha! tricked ya, old mind, old pal) just to be still, quiet, and to be able to rest into our already completely "still" natural organically Innocent Primacy of Divine Ecstasy. We must just rest, just drop from the wild and hectic, maddening confusion of all-center internal warfare, from the vast profusion of contradictory "I's," to the quietude of the unity of the truth of our already present, already

Enlightened selves. What, in our lives, most easefully allows this state to be expressed?

Well, stodginess, of course. The stodgy man is already disposed to such Realization. He moves slowly, he lives with the least amount of exactitude, he denies distraction from his stodginess. It is much too much effort for the stodgy man to direct his energy and attention anywhere, let alone to allow any active and enthusiastic involvement by them. So you see that realistically, one who is overcome by middle age stodginess is quite readily available—primed one might say—for the Revelation of the Primacy of Natural Ecstasy, the effortless and intentionless manifestation of Organic Innocence. The battle of the bulge (an organic middle-aged phenomenon), once surrendered to (and why not, since it *is* organically programmed into the organism); the phenomena of grey hair, once recognized as a movement into regality instead of as a sign of "age" (as in old and crotchety); and the unfortunate realization that Rock and Roll (of the Punk and Heavy Metal sort of course, not Real R&R) is really just noise, all give way to the acceptance of the presence and overwhelming character of *stodginess.* And once accepted, once Realized in its entirety and its implications, stodginess must give way to the Great Divine Revelation of silence, or Stillness. Such a Revelation paves the way for a delicious second half of life and an Enlightened disposition from then on. There is such equanimity to stodginess, after all.

But the embrace of the middle aged stodgy condition is not merely the empty philosophical acceptance that life is what it is and we might as well deal with it, and after all, all things change and we can't do anything about it anyway, all the time having a raging dissatisfaction beneath the surface unconsciously building towards the destruction of this sterile philosophy in an explosion of late middle-aged terror and fear, smashing the smug "acceptance of God's contributions, whatever they are" attitude of so many new age boors who assume there is no Work to do. No, I must say two times, No. To embrace organic stodginess is not to assume a weak and hollow philosophy about life, but it is to know so actually and so consumingly that life is as it is, as to make the obvious, and the illusory, impotent. The stodgy man knows what must be done for God; knows what is submission to the great Process of Divine Evolution, and knows the Truth of the Work because none of his energy and attention is wasted, frittered away on useless wishes (like for his hair to get thicker again, or for his muscle tone to be like it was at twenty-two, or for his pecker to only last three and a half minutes before spitting, etc...) The stodgy man Rests; his sloth is his glory, his rootedness is his majesty. His energy and attention are absorbed in the placid pool of his organically Innocent state: stodginess. What a blessing to look forward to if you are still young and vibrant, spewing the fire of your brilliant energy in all directions like the flopping filaments of a fibre-optic rainlight. The stodgy man is One, he is sole, he is not divided, not splintered. His vision is complete, honed to a steady, stodgy stillness. That is the wonderful destiny that middle age holds, if only we might have the clarity to appreciate it for what it is. I toast middle age! To the stodgy man! Skol!

The following books are available through Hohm Press:

This book contains the crucial sutras to the teaching Work of Lee Lozowick. It includes his definitive statement of non-dualism—"The Divine Path of Growing Old," the forerunner of his teaching on Loving God—"For the Love of God," and other important essays such as "The Divine Road of Reactional Enquiry."

Laughter of the Stones is recommended as the introductory text to this Way. It makes the most basic statements of the radical nature of our Teaching, an understanding of which is essential to further participation.

Paperback, 140 pages, $3.94

In the Fire is the foundation teaching text of the Hohm Community. It contains the most comprehensive description of actually working with a spiritual Master, consisting of transcripts of talks given by Lee Lozowick prior to 1978. These talks cover the fundamentals of practice, the details of the movement of Divine Influence, and concise descriptions of the process of ego.

Along with *Laughter of the Stones* and *The Only Grace is Loving God, In the Fire* completes the essential Teaching material.

Paperback, 241 pages, $5.95

The Only Grace is Loving God is unlike any other spiritual book available on the market today. Written in ecstatic speech, it proclaims that "Loving God" is a Gift, the only Gift given by God to mankind. It is the most radical statement ever made about the relationship of "Personal God" and "Impersonal God" to man.

Any serious student of spiritual or religious studies will recognize that a revelatory statement is being made. This book resolves the age-old conflict of dualism versus non-dualism with a leap in perspective. *The Only Grace is Loving God* is Lee Lozowick's special and uniquely individual offering.

Paperback, 94 pages, $5.95

The *Divine Slave Gita* is the bi-monthly magazine we publish as the principal vehicle for the communication of our Teaching. For further information on subscriptions, other continuing educational services and participation in the different levels of involvement, please write:

Correspondence Department
Hohm
P.O. Box 25839
Prescott Valley, Arizona 86312